praise for billy goodnick

"It's about time Billy put his considerable expertise and irreverent voice into a book everyone can benefit from. Funny, blunt and insightful – his is a rare and refreshing voice in the world of garden writing."

– Steve Aitken, editor, Fine Gardening *magazine*

"Billy is the expert you want in your corner if you've got a yard that needs help. His unique talent is designing sustainable, low-maintenance gardens that are beautiful as well as highly livable...and showing how anyone can do it too."

– Joe Lamp'l, host and executive producer of "Growing a Greener World"

"There are times when Billy Goodnick's design advice makes me laugh out loud – how often can you say that about a gardening book? Smart and sassy, Billy is entirely successful as an educator who also entertains...guaranteed to change the way you think about your own backyard."

– Debra Prinzing, author of Slow Flowers *and co-creator of* The 50 Mile Bouquet

"There really is no one else like Billy, who combines solid horticultural and design knowledge with wit, humor and a natural ability to write well."

– Debra Lee Baldwin, garden photojournalist and author of Designing with Succulents *and* Succulent Container Gardens

"Billy Goodnick: Landscape architect, master educator, brilliant humorist. Earmark some space in your bookcase for this writer – you'll want all his future books!"

– Shirley Bovshow, TV producer and host

yards

turn any outdoor space
into the garden of
your dreams

billy goodnick

st. lynn's
press

PITTSBURGH

Yards
Turn any Outdoor Space into the Garden of Your Dreams

ISBN-13: 978-0-9855622-1-2

5162 1455 6/13

Library of Congress Control Number: 2012940816
CIP information available upon request

First Edition, 2013

St. Lynn's Press . POB 18680 . Pittsburgh, PA 15236
412.466.0790 . www.stlynnspress.com

Book design – Holly Rosborough
Editor – Catherine Dees

Photographs © Billy Goodnick
Page preceding table of contents, xiv, xvi, xviii, 2, 5, 6, 7, 8, 10, 13, 14, 15, 16, 23, 25 top, 26,
27, 28, 34, 36, 38, 39, 40, 41, 42, 45, 47, 49, 50, 56, 57 top, 58, 60 bottom, 62, 64, 72, 73, 74 top,
76 top, 77 top, 78, 79, 80, 83, 85 all, 86 all, 88, 92, 93, 94, 96 top and middle, 97 top, 98,
100 all, 101 all, 102, 104, 106, 108 bottom, 110 top, 116, 119, 120, 122, 123, 126, 139

Photographs by others are credited on page 141.

Illustrations © Billy Goodnick

Printed in Canada
on certified FSC recycled paper using soy-based inks

This title and all of St. Lynn's Press books may be purchased for educational,
business, or sales promotional use. For information please write:
Special Markets Department . St. Lynn's Press . POB 18680 . Pittsburgh, PA 15236

10 9 8 7 6 5 4 3 2 1

This book is dedicated to…

❧

Lin, my wife, who continually says,
"Whatever makes you happy."

❧

Benjamin Cosmo, my poet son, who says
"You *go,* daddio."

❧

Biff the Wonder Spaniel

table of contents

introduction

The Good Yard

A good yard doesn't just happen. You've got to work for it. I'm not talking about digging holes, defending against varmints, or hauling wheelbarrows of topsoil up near-vertical goat trails. That might come later. The work I'm talking about starts between your ears – it's the calories you burn listening for what your yard is trying to tell you. I should know. I've been listening to yards, rescuing unhappy ones and designing new ones for nearly four decades. Optimist that I am, I believe that any outdoor space can be a good yard...not only that, it can graduate from being just a "yard" to being a place that serves your family's lifestyle year-round.

First things first

There are two things I insist on from any landscape I design, and you should too:

First: A good yard has got to be beautiful. Sure, the Big B is in the eyes of the beholder. For some folks it's a garden populated with Pepto-pink flamingos; who am I to argue? (Well, actually, in later chapters I'll get my rant on about the atrocities perpetrated in the name of horticulture.) But that won't stop me from trying to convince you that there are some simple, universal aesthetic principles of garden design that can make you a lot happier with your yard.

Second: Just like a teenager, a good yard needs to do more than just sit there looking cool. For all the time and money you'll put into designing, installing and caring for a yard, it had better give something back. I expect a good yard to be an extension of the home, providing places for connecting with family and friends, star gazing, growing good grub (not grubs), and playing fetch with your pet iguana.

And another thing...

A good yard ascribes to what I call the Horticultural Hippocratic Oath: Do No Harm. Good yards consume fewer natural resources, excrete fewer toxic by-products, and they're quieter too (think gas-powered mowers). They brim with diversity, attracting hungry beneficial insects. They tap the waste stream and often resurrect building materials that still have long, useful lives ahead of them. They are low maintenance and low cost. Did I mention, they're beautiful?

Somebody did this on purpose!

A Bad Yard

I'm guessing you picked up this book because there are a few things about your landscape you'd like to improve. Maybe "bad" isn't quite the right word for your yard, but "good" might be a bit of a stretch. Again, I'm just guessing. That's okay. I've seen it all, and I can promise you that "good" is within your reach. A bad yard can wreak havoc on relationships and, at the very least, ruin weekends. You know something's wrong, but you can't agree on how to fix it. Things die, nothing looks right, the lawn is a war zone, it's too hot to read a book and your friends are making excuses not to come over for cookouts. If any of this touches a nerve, your yard isn't doing what yards should do: be your refuge...and be beautiful.

Who Needs This Book?

I don't pretend to have written the definitive book of garden design. What I have penned, though, is the book I think everyone should read before they go out and buy all those other books – you know, the ones that will fill in the details about how to measure your property, install a brick walkway, engineer an efficient sprinkler system, or suggest the best plants for your particular gardening zone. But for the moment, leave your gold card in your wallet – what you need to get started is in your hands.

You know a professionally designed landscape when you see it. The job of *YARDS* is to demystify how it got that way. It asks the big questions that the best designers consider before they put a line on the plan or name the plants that will make your entryway sing. I'm going to equip you with a logical process you can follow that will put you at ease.

I've written this book for three kinds of readers:

- The Generalist: I'm hoping to squirt a shot of brain lube between your ears to help you re-imagine your property.
- The Do-It-Yourselfer (and the subspecies, *Homo over-achieverensis*): You intend to take on all phases of design and installation. YARDS promises the knowledge and confidence boost you'll need to create a gorgeous, useful garden you'll enjoy every day. And if you bite off more than you can chew, I've left you a nice Appendix section that tells you who to call for expert assistance.
- The Informed Consumer: You will probably end up hiring a professional designer, but need help sorting out priorities, defining your expectations and refining your eye.

And when you get to the end of the book, I've prepared a list of resources to cover all the stuff I didn't have room for earlier.

What's Inside

Part 1: Design. Part 1 lays out the big picture, demonstrating how to get your head around all the opportunities and constraints your property presents, and encouraging you to think hard about how to get the most out of your space. You'll sharpen your observation skills and brainstorm all the things you'd like to be able to do in your outdoor spaces. I'll help you define your personal style and determine how much space for all your activities. And if you enjoyed scribbling in coloring books when you were a kid, I'll show you how to brainstorm on paper.

Part 2: Aesthetics. Part 2 is all about pleasing your senses. You know what you like when you see it, but can you translate that to your own garden? I'll teach you how to figure that one out. I'll help you master the fundamentals of visual design, deal with three-dimensional space and refine your grasp of color theory. And since gardens continually evolve, I'll share how four-season thinking will increase your enjoyment.

Part 3: Hardscape. Part 3 starts by showing how outdoor spaces can be thought of as more rooms of your house, with their own unique floors, walls, and sometimes, ceilings – then highlight the wide range of materials at your disposal. I dig down and show you the important but often-unseen infrastructure of a fully functional landscape: the pipes, utilities, and hardware that make a good landscape work. And I encourage you to call for help when a job is beyond your skill set.

Part 4: Plants. Part 4 takes you through my four-step plant selection process, starting with the practical role plants can play, while assuring that the plants you select will stick around for a long time. Then the real fun starts – creating beautiful plant combinations that range from subtle to stunning. If you've drooled over dreamy gardens in magazines but had trouble figuring out how to use that inspiration in your own garden, I've got that covered, too.

And I can't write a book without poking a wee bit of educational fun, with a few pages of *Crimes Against Horticulture: When Bad Taste Meets Power Tools,* my twisted look at the amazingly boneheaded, f'ugly things people do in the name of gardening.

The Long and Winding Road

A good yard isn't a product, it's a process. The good news and bad news is that a garden is never done: Shade happens, gophers git yer gladiolus, kids outgrow swing sets, tastes change. But when you make it to the end of this book and start putting the key ideas to work for you, I promise you'll have a yard that will meet your needs for years to come.

For fear of contradicting my first statement, good yards do happen if you learn the basics, free your imagination, and head down the garden path one stepping stone at a time.

PART 1

design

You gotta have a plan

A good yard can change your life. You may not be able to define what makes a good yard right now, but you know one when you see it. I'll let you in on a secret: That appealing arrangement of plants and other stuff didn't get there without someone giving it a whole lot of thought. The best, most user-friendly outdoor spaces come from following a logical process, starting with big dreams and working toward the details. You wouldn't design a new house by starting with the fabric swatches for the throw pillows, and you don't design a garden by popping into the nursery and filling your trunk with flashy flowers. First things first. If you're OK with that, then let's get designing!

CHAPTER 1

analysis

What do you have to work with?

*D*esigning a great garden is an exercise in problem solving that starts with identifying opportunities and constraints, then moves on to observing, assessing, and refining your goals. These critical, early steps will save you big bucks later and result in a garden you'll love for years. It pays to look at what you have to work with and where you want to go – and to anticipate the obstacles that could get in your way. The more you can do that upfront, before you start picking out the plants and moving dirt, the fewer bumps you're likely to hit down the road. Knowledge is power.

Get to Know Your Site

Imagine you're a garden designer hired to resuscitate someone's tired, old landscape. Even over the phone, something seems strange: They won't let you visit the site, won't even tell you which state they live in. What are the odds you can meet their needs? Zip. To develop an intelligent plan of action you would need to know a whole lot about their site. The same goes for your own yard. You need to get in touch with your site: Walk the area, taking a good look at everything, then make a rough sketch. It works for me and I know it will work for you. That sketch will become your starting point for the eventual design.

This isn't an art project; it's just for reference, as in down-and-dirty. When I do this, I return to the site a number of times, to really get a feel for the space as a whole…and for its issues.

graph paper (a few pieces)
pencil (and an eraser – nobody's perfect)
clipboard
camera and/or video camera

Hang onto these items. They're the foundation of your Home Design Studio (Appendix B) Your freehand sketch should show the bare minimum of information, because the more detail you show about what's already there, the harder it will be to imagine something different.

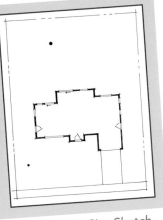

Your Basic Site Sketch

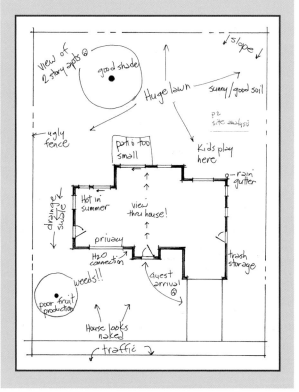

Site Analysis Sketch

What to do

First, draw the outline of the house and garage, show property lines, swimming pool, major trees you're pretty certain you'll be leaving – and that's about it. Even if you think you'd never jackhammer out your current walkway or patio, allow yourself to imagine what your yard would be like if you had the total freedom to reshape or relocate things. Give your imagination a clean canvas.

(Once you've drawn your basic site sketch, make a copy or two because you'll need it later on in your design process.)

Now take another walk. Clear your mind. Stroll through your yard and observe your thoughts. When you see something you think is relevant to your future garden, jot it down at the corresponding location on your map. You might want to expand your comments on a fresh sheet of paper as well.

Record objective stuff, the things you can quantify and count: dead lawn, areas where the downspouts flood the beds, windy areas, the barren front door bed, maintenance "black holes" that suck the life out of your spare time, unsafe paving.

Express your subjective reactions; the way you feel about your current yard: not enough privacy from the neighbors; it's inconvenient to get to your tools; no real style or color scheme, color schemes that don't work.

Take panoramic photos from multiple vantage points. In addition to taking regular photos, I like using video, because I can walk and talk at the same time, which leads to on-the-spot ideas I want to capture. And I won't have to stop and make notes.

Sit awhile. When you think you're done and you've seen all there is to be seen, grab a folding chair and just sit in different parts of the garden, especially those you don't usually frequent. If you've been unhappy with your yard for a long time, there are probably places you just don't want to linger in, but do it anyway. Do this at different times of day. You'll be surprised by what you discover and how your design thinking expands. (You might want to recall how these places felt at other times of the year, not just the present season.) Don't rush. This is going to be an organic progression of ideas and inspiration.

More things to look for and respond to:

- Paths: Are the ones you have doing the job? Are they havens for weeds?
- Storage: enough, not enough, in the wrong place?
- Plants you like/don't like: no time for sentiment here
- Drainage patterns: Where are the problem places? You want runoff to flow away from the house and not through the bedroom.
- Erodible or unstable slopes
- Hot spots: including interior of house, where there's no shading from outside
- Favorite places to hang out

Beautiful stonework to highlight

Plants to help, plants to remove

- Street issues: Do car lights or street lights bother you at night? Do you need a noise buffer?
- Eyesores: semi-permanent things like ugly chain-link fence
- Unusual soil conditions
- Zombie nesting areas

When you're done, set the site analysis, map and notes aside or file them in your Home Design Studio. These become the base camp from which you'll journey forward.

Needs Assessment: What do you want to *do* when you go outside?

You've seen and analyzed what your site has to tell you. Now let's look at how you plan to enjoy your new garden, and how it's going to fit your family's lifestyle.

I want my clients to get the most from the time and money they invest. I want to meet their needs, and so I ask a lot of seemingly nosy questions to stimulate well-considered responses. I start with the most fundamental question for creating a great yard: "What do you want to *do* when you go outside?"

Outdoors as an extension of your house: "Form follows function" is a tried and true adage in every design discipline, and it applies to planning a good yard. Maybe there are people out there so hooked on gardening that as long as something's in bloom they're thrilled. But for my money (and the people I design for), outdoor spaces should be an extension of the house, only chlorophyll-ier. As long as you're paying property taxes on that real estate, shouldn't it reward you with more than a sore back?

Create spaces that enhance your lifestyle

In the list below are some self-evaluation questions to get your creative juices flowing, but I'm sure you'll think of more. Grab another sheet of paper; here we go again.

- Do you eat outdoors? How often? On what scale?
- Do you like to cook/barbecue outdoors?
- Do you want a meditation/reading area?
- Do you plan on growing food? On what scale?
- Do you want a cutting garden?
- Do you and your family like to play outdoors? Pool? Hot tub? Basketball? Croquet? Easter egg hunts?
- Do you need a place to store your outdoor stuff? How big, what kind of access?

- Does your family have mobility/disability concerns?
- Will your maintenance be DIY or a gardening service?
- Is water and resource conservation important to you?

Evaluating your needs will tell you a lot about where you want to go with your design. When you're done, file it.

Constraints: What's stopping you?

When my son, Cosmo, was going through the Terrible Twos, every day was an adventure in challenging the rules. I'm glad he wasn't designing landscapes at that age. I can just see the look on his client's face as he wails, "But I don't WANNA observe the zoning ordinance requiring that a fence in the front yard be 42 inches or lower!!!"

A storage shed in plain view should contribute to the beauty of your yard

Legal stuff: Like it or not, there are limits on what you can do with your yard. Some constraints are of a legal nature, like zoning laws that keep your neighbor from building a drag strip in their side yard. There are building codes assuring that it's safe to slam a door without fear of the house collapsing.

In the garden, many of these same rules apply, varying throughout different states, counties, and cities. It's best to do your homework and find out which ones apply to your project as soon as possible. What do I mean? Let's say you've been dreaming about a beautifully crafted stone wall around your new patio. You've already contacted a local stonemason to build it. He comes highly recommended; what could go wrong? Lots. If you know the zoning law "trigger" between a DIY stone wall and one requiring a professional engineer, you'll be able to adjust your ambitions to keep your project simple and inexpensive. Ignore the rules and you could face fines and the expense of ripping out your beautiful new wall and replacing it.

Climate: Climate is a constraint you can manipulate to some degree, but there are limits. Good luck growing saguaro cacti along the shores of Lake Superior. The smarter, sustainable approach to landscaping is picking plants that want to grow where you put them, instead of putting them on life-support for their survival. And climate will affect your comfort both indoors and outside.

Budget: Nineteenth century architect and planner, Daniel Burnham got it right, declaring, "Make no little plans; they have no magic to stir men's blood and probably themselves will not be realized. Make big plans; aim high in hope and work."

The Rolling Stones were a little more blunt: "You can't always get what you want."

What I love about designing gardens is the problem-solving aspect of it – the challenge of balancing the practical, aesthetic, and environmental desires with the reality of limitations.

It doesn't cost anything to dream big; you can always take a reality pill later. I think your primary concern at this early stage in the design process should be considering all the outdoor rooms and features that will make your life more fun and beautiful. Once you have a big plan, you can simplify the design, tackle it in bite-size chunks, or execute with simpler materials.

The analysis phase of the design is done, but not forgotten. Like a crime scene investigator (but without the stiletto heels or rock-hard abs), you've scoured your surroundings with clipboard and camera. You've got your bullet lists. You've bribed the family with pizza long enough to have them sit still and brainstorm all manner of possibilities with you.

Design Steps

There are so many steps to designing a garden that I thought it might be helpful at this point to zoom out and give you the big picture.

Everyone's garden needs are different, so you'll probably find yourself picking and choosing from this master check list. This will help you understand the process, order of operations, as well as the terminology I use in this book. Other professional designers might use different systems and vocabulary, but this road map should help get you rolling.

Design Development – where it all begins

- **Site analysis** – the opportunities and constraints of your site and surrounding
- **Needs assessment** – what you'd like from your garden
- **Definition** – figuring out what it all means and setting your course

Planning – giving form to your idea

- **Bubble diagrams** – visual brainstorming of different configurations
- **Schematic plan** – defining the forms and spaces in a general way
- **Planting concept** – general locations and massings of plants
- **Plant palette development** – generating and refining the plants you'll use
- **Final plan** – detailed refinement of constructed elements (grading, drainage, paving, irrigation, lighting, walls, etc.) and final plant choices and locations.

Construction – putting your ideas on (and in) the ground

- **Site preparation** – demolition, grading, drainage
- **Hardscape** – all the above-ground building: patios, paths, walls, gazebos, fountains, etc.
- **Planting preparation** – soil conditioning and amendment, final grading, irrigation
- **Planting** – the easy part
- **Clean-up** – making the yard useable
- **Maintenance** – getting plants established, then meeting their ongoing needs for trimming, feeding, and weed and pest control using safe, sustainable practices.

You'll be meeting most of these steps in more or less detail throughout the book.

A World of Possibilities

There's probably no end to all the things you could pack into a landscape, from miniature railways to a giant water slide. I'll leave it to you to stretch the limits, but here's my brain-dump of useful spaces, amenities and ideas worth considering before finalizing your design. Plug in a few as keyword searches on your computer, then click "images" and see if anything cool pops up…

Kids' Play: swing, climber, sandbox, safe fall-surfacing, wet play, trike track, skate ramp, butterfly garden, tree house, bean-pole tent, camping, miniature golf, chalk art, mud, trampoline, tumbling, gymnastics, wading pool, room to throw or kick a ball or toss a Frisbee

Pets: soft paths for dogs to race on, graceful grasses for cats to bat about, sunny spots to nap, covered places to get out of the rain, poisonous plants to avoid (check with ASPCA or your vet)

Homesteading: veggie beds, potting table, composting, orchard, edible ornamentals, cutting flowers/roses, herbs, vertical gardens, greenhouse, bee-keeping, chickens

Nature: attractors for butterflies, bees, beneficial insects and hummingbirds, bird feeders, bird bath, nesting material, shelter, native plants, nesting boxes, nature trail, critter-proofing, fish, frogs

Activities: dining, cooking, serving, sleeping, playing, sipping, hobbies, sports, soaking, swimming, horseshoes, croquet, lawn bowling

Ambiance/décor: lighting (electrical, gas, candle), fragrance, pavilion, privacy, mystery, audio, noise-masking, misting, fireplace/fire pit, gas heating, water feature, art/sculpture, shade structure/shade sail/umbrella, container garden, bench, chair, table, hammock, day bed

Practical: storage, outdoor shower, trash enclosure, dog run, parking, security, privacy, bug-proofing, wind-screen

Safety: grading, drainage, firescaping, slip-resistance, visibility, handrails, pollen/allergies, retaining wall, pool enclosure, plant toxicity (humans and pets), slope retention

Sustainability: water conservation, "smart" irrigation controllers, native plants, organic gardening, integrated pest management, recycled/reused materials, storm water run-off, water harvesting, green roof, local materials, fossil fuel-free tools, composting, permaculture

The Design Starts Here: the Now What? drawing

"I did the analysis, but now I've got a lot of conflicting information. Can't I just start picking out my plants?" Not so fast, Buster. This is when the creative design process really starts, responding with your gut reaction to everything you've observed and recorded so far. It's time to summarize the volumes of input and consider how to address the issues you've raised. Most likely, the analysis alerted you to opportunities you hadn't considered, and constraints that you'll have to overcome or adapt to.

What I call the Now What? drawing is based on the same sketch you used for the site analysis – that simple, pared down drawing of your yard, minus most of the stuff you'll want to consider changing. (That's why I asked you to make copies of your original site map before you marked it up.)

For example, if you noted in your analysis that the front bedroom lacks privacy, do not respond on the Now What? drawing with "Plant six hydrangeas in a curving, 12-foot long by

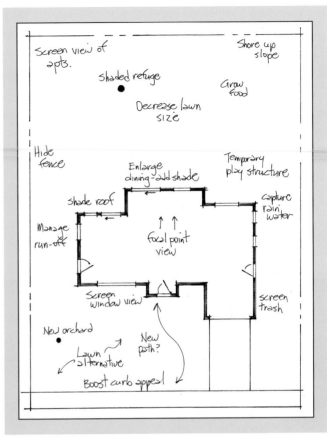

After analyzing your site and needs, record your gut reaction

6-foot wide bed using a backfill mix of three parts native soil and one part fir bark compost." Do that and you've squashed any other possibility, like installing a vine-covered trellis instead, or converting your yard to an orchard, or making the entire space into an enclosed courtyard with a bubbling fountain. Simple and obvious as it seems, just jot a note on the drawing, in the general geographic area, stating your intention to "Make yard more private." The final decision of how you'll do that comes later.

Look at my Now What? drawing on this page. It was done on a clean copy of the sketch I used for a client's site analysis. You'll see the general idea.

For your own Now What? drawing, your objective is to respond to all the data – objective and subjective – that you've accumulated. This is important: Your responses need to remain vague and open-ended, because if you start fussing with the details too soon, you'll stifle those creative juices. You might miss the possibility of choosing from a variety of solutions, some better than your first flash of brilliance.

Continue making notes on the drawing, capturing your instinctive first thoughts. If you know your family wants a place for entertaining larger groups, write: "Enlarge dining patio for 10-person sit-down dining." Need a place to read the Sunday funnies? Add a note near the big shade tree: "Chillax-a-torium."

When you're done, look the drawing over and stash it in your Home Design Studio. There's a good chance your final design will incorporate a lot of these solutions. But you don't want to close the door on that lightning bolt that's going to wake you up in the middle of the night. Good design needs a relaxed, gestational period.

So, while it's gestating, let's talk style for a while.

CHAPTER 2

finding your style

If it makes you smile (and nobody gets hurt), I'm fine with that

*H*ere's a bad idea: You live in a house that looks like it belongs on France's Normandy coast. You're intending to landscape the yard with your Sonoran desert cactus collection. This odd combo might look nice to you, but don't expect any style awards. Granted, there's probably not a vigilante brigade from the Crimes Against Horticulture squad in your neighborhood waiting to publicly shame you. But, like chocolate milk and sardines, some things just shouldn't mix it up.

When we talk about "garden style" we generally mean a garden emblematic of a particular historic period and geographic region. Examples: Mediterranean-style gardens reflect the influences of Islam and the Moorish culture: conservative use of scarce water, simple floral color schemes, and water-thrifty plants arranged to reinforce a symmetrical layout of the grounds. Japanese gardens embody the Shinto religion's animist belief that nature is imbued with spirit. Based on this philosophy, they create gardens showing reverence for natural elements.

Style Guidelines

I think that if you live in a house with a distinct architectural style, you have a higher obligation to marry the garden to the house. Take a weekend bike ride and look at other homes like yours. You'll notice gardens that just seem to "fit" the house, and ones that clash. Chances are, the ones you like follow the design principles of that historic design period. A Federalist house will have symmetrical walks, rose beds, perennial borders; a 50s Modern uses strong angles, high-contrast and sculptural plantings.

Strive for simplicity in gardens around traditional homes

On the other hand, if figuring out the style of your home leaves you scratching your head and running to the nearest architectural historian, don't fret. A house that doesn't make a strong style statement frees you to try on different styles without causing a visual train wreck of conflicting concepts. Like the ubiquitous white-painted walls of an art museum, there's no conflict if one gallery exhibits the wildness of a Jackson Pollack free-for-all and another houses the more restrained work of the Italian Renaissance.

And then there's the Eclectic garden, whimsically grabbing bits and pieces from different styles. It's strictly a matter of personal taste whether you want to go in this direction, regardless of the architecture. Sometimes it's the landscaping style people call the "mix-and-match" approach that doesn't fit neatly into a category. That's okay. Some of my favorite garden designs defy labeling. But every day they bring joy to their owners and to visitors. Sometimes a client apologizes to me for not being more committed to a particular look or style. I put them at ease. "You're the one who lives here. If it makes you smile (and nobody gets hurt), I'm cool with that."

In the Aesthetics section of this book I'll spell out the basic principles of visual design, to fine tune your eye and inspire you. These will help you to better understand how styles are created and how to adapt these statements to your own yard.

Another approach to creating the garden of your dreams is to think in terms of themes.

Selecting a Theme

Weaving a consistent theme through your garden adds an extra dimension to your yard. Like a musical motif that comes and goes, expressed in a slightly different way each time it appears, a theme ties the garden together and generates anticipation for the next reveal. As you'll see, most themes can exist within any style of garden.

Water: One of the most common themes used in garden design is water. For every style of garden there are traditional ways to incorporate water. As cited earlier, Mediterranean-influenced gardens use water with great reverence, due to its scarcity. At the center of the patio, water is expressed as a barely bubbling fountain surrounded by a simple geometric pool. Elsewhere, perhaps in a secluded refuge, a birdbath provides another expression of water.

In contrast, a woodland garden might feature water as a gently flowing stream. You don't even need real water to make a statement: In a desert landscape, a dried arroyo with artfully arranged boulders and rocks tells us that water has shaped the garden, but isn't always present.

Movement: You can create a feeling of movement with a series of paths that transport you through the garden, revealing outdoor rooms and vistas in a game of hide and seek. Movement also includes plants that are animated by breezes, like tall ornamental grasses, or clattering columns of bamboo.

Art: I'm not going to try to define garden art here. For some folks, classically inspired works in marble serve as magnets that draw visitors along the paths and through the garden. For others, displaying their grandkids' hand-painted bird houses on the fence outside the family room does the trick. Next thing you know, the yard becomes dappled with youthful expression and fun. Collections of found objects can be organized in a series of "galleries," with each exhibition embellished with plants to suit the mood.

Art can be the center of attention, or teasing from behind a spray of foliage. Practical items like seating, lights, handrails, and gates can be turned into works of art, in the right hands. Though these will likely cost more than mass-produced plastic lawn chairs, they can elevate your garden to a higher aesthetic level and personalize it. Funk is art, too – look for things you can pull from the waste stream, then soak them in a bowl of imagination overnight.

Nature: If you want your garden to attract desirable wildlife, consider bird feeders, beneficial insect-attractors, native plants, water, and lightly managed tangles of brush.

Color: You can play with color by designing different parts of the garden based on a dominant color scheme – like a blue garden with restful morning colors, a hot-colored garden that comes to life in midday sun, or a white garden glowing on moonlit nights.

There are many other thematic elements that make a garden sing. Take a garden tour, flip through magazines, or cruise websites for other themes that excite you. We'll consider some of them as we go along.

Allow yourself the freedom to imagine many style possibilities, not only the ones that you're used to. Now's the moment to put everything on the table.

CHAPTER 3

planning your outdoor living

Climate, 'Rooms,' Entertainment, Privacy, Places for Your Stuff, Safety

A poorly designed yard is like a lopsided relationship, with one partner doing all the giving and the other expecting more. Other than suck the soul out of your precious weekends running laps behind a belching mower, what has your yard done for you lately? What has it given back besides pollen, a runny nose and more work?

In my worldview, pretty flowers are cool, but the highest purpose of a yard is living in it. Time to pull out your needs assessment list and think about what your yard can contribute to the relationship.

The first time through the needs assessment I suggested that you "make no small plans." I hope you didn't pull your punches, but instead let your imagination run amok. Hopefully, you've identified ideas to help you get more out of your yard.

But choices will need to be made, grand schemes rescaled, wish lists pared down, materials simplified. What do you hang onto and fight for, and what do you cut loose? I find it's helpful to rank your wish list based first on your passion for each item, not the perceived cost or difficulty to accomplish. Better to preserve the activity and do it on a budget, than give up on it completely.

Know Your Local Climate and Microclimate

One thing that can't be ignored as you plan your ideal outdoor spaces is the climate you live in. Weather happens. But there are ways to coax nature to work with you.

For every region in the country, there are general climate patterns we can predict (though given what we've seen of global climate change, nothing's a sure bet). Winters in the central states can be bitterly cold, while along the Left Coast I'm wearing shorts and flip flops. There's the dry, lizard-friendly summer heat of Tucson, and a day's drive east serves up enough humidity to make you dredge yourself in a tub of talcum powder.

The USDA divides the country into climate zones, based on average low temperatures, painted with a broad brush. It's good, basic information for determining which plants will have the best survival rates in your garden, but it's not the whole picture. You'll be a lot more successful if you learn to recognize the conditions that define your particular micro-climate – the many subtle, but important differences that will affect

USDA plant hardiness map,
http://planthardiness.ars.
usda.gov/PHZMWeb

your yard and how you approach its design. All yards have more than one microclimate, making it all the more important to be aware of some climatic facts of life.

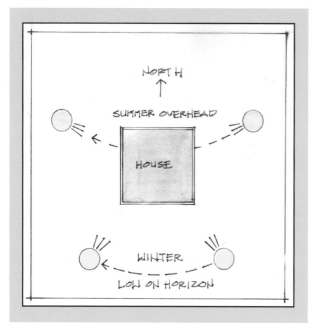

Summer sun rises in the northeast, sets northwest and tracks overhead.

Microclimate affects human comfort as well as plant growth. It influences where you place your living areas. It can be modified through planted and constructed features. Some things to be aware of:

Sun patterns: They change throughout the year, so it's important to know where to place trees and structures to capture light and warmth in winter and give you shade in summer. It helps to know the aspect, or direction a slope faces, a factor in sun intensity (southwest aspect bakes in afternoon heat, while northern aspect receives the sun's glancing rays, even at high noon).

Air flow: Because warm air rises and cold air sinks, low spots will be more prone to frost and uncomfortable to occupy in cooler weather. Wind chill can make two parts of the property very different for entertaining purposes. Wind can be directed and filtered through proper plantings and structure shapes.

Surfaces: Masonry walls and dark paving absorb, then radiate heat slowly as temps drop (good in winter, harsh in hot weather). Light colors, windows and flat water reflect sunlight; they also produce glare.

Whatever microclimates you have to work with, good design takes advantage of its benefits and minimizes its negatives.

Rooms

I'm betting that most of the things you listed in your needs assessment will require specialized spaces. Did "Throw more al fresco dining parties" top your list? Sure, you could carry your dining room chairs to the back lawn and eat beans from the can, but that's not anyone's idea of a great yard. And then there are the kids: Creating fun, safe places for the little folks requires intelligent and imaginative planning, with options that might include a lawn for tumbling and sprinkler play, a climbing structure, discovery garden, playhouse, trike track, or portable pool. Think long-term: Once the kids are older, out of the yard and on the soccer field, the tot lot might make a great future place for a secluded hot tub.

A Concept Statement for Every Room

Designing a landscape isn't something most people do every day. You've got a list of cool ideas, but how do you sharpen your focus so you know which path to follow?

Inside the house, your dining room is arranged and furnished for meals and family games. But when it's time to get lost in a good book, straight-back chairs and glass tabletops don't cut it. You'll want to chill out on the couch or a comfy chair. Same goes in the garden: Different activities need specialized rooms and furnishings.

The most efficient approach to clarifying your goals and getting what you want is by composing a series of concept statements, one for each room in the garden. A concept statement is like a goal, only more specific; like an objective, but more vague. It consists of three pieces of information:

- What *happens* in the room
- What it *feels* like to be in the space
- In a general way, what the room *looks* like

Let's look inside my brain as I design my ideal garden refuge.

Here's how it would work for me in designing my own yard: I'm more of a slug than a lizard when it comes to my ideal climate. During the needs assessment, I decided that I would love to have a quiet getaway spot. My ideal garden refuge would fit the following description: "A cool, secluded, forested clearing where I can close my eyes and listen to birds." In one sentence, I've declared my intentions and given myself a clear goal. I think I hit three bull's-eyes:

- ⚙ **What's the space for?** *Relaxing and communing with nature.*
- ⚙ **What does it feel like when I'm in there?** *Cool and secluded.*
- ⚙ **What does it look like?** *A forest clearing.*

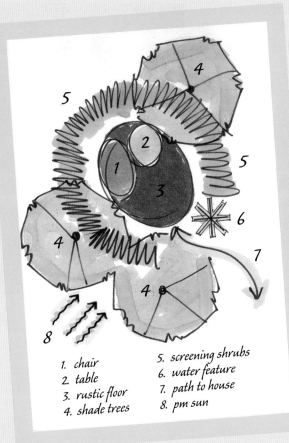

1. chair
2. table
3. rustic floor
4. shade trees
5. screening shrubs
6. water feature
7. path to house
8. pm sun

I've just eliminated a few hundred possible alternative designs, saving myself time and clarifying the big idea. It won't be a rock garden, a swimming pool or a veggie plot. What I will need is a path, plants, and a place to park my keister.

Ooops. Reality check. 1) My yard is in the middle of sub-urbia, not the Berkshires; 2) I can see every inch of my yard from anywhere on the property; 3) The place feels like Death Valley on summer afternoons.

Sure, I've got some work to do, but at least now I can set some objectives.

I'll plant a bed of tall shrubs between me and the rest of the yard, include a couple of shade trees (young or mature, depending on my budget, so this might take a few years), and size the space to accommodate a well-padded chair and a small table for my stuff. If I want to take it a step further, I'll add a bird feeder nearby and include a source of running water.

That's the beauty of a concept statement: With one sentence, I've bypassed all the distracting possibilities that won't suit my needs.

Once you've got your concept statement for each garden room in priority order, it's time to consider the other amenities that make these spaces useful. (We'll talk about how to actually arrange these rooms in the section "Bubbling with Options.")

Sizing your space: being realistic

It stands to reason that a practical, comfortable bedroom needs to be bigger than just the footprint of your bed. You see where I'm going with this? Your outdoor rooms should be sized for not only the necessary furnishings, but also with extra space to move around – and room for a few fun baubles to give it personality.

This is why doing a concept statement exercise pays off. For example, if you imagined your secret refuge as a place just big enough for you, you might only need room for a comfortable chair to sink into. But it would be a lot more useful if you had a small, flat boulder next to it for an ice tea and the Sunday crossword puzzle.

So how much room do you need? Most outdoor spaces have an equivalent room inside your house:

- patio = dining room
- refuge = den
- morning terrace = breakfast nook
- vegetable garden = that room where you haven't swept up for a few decades

Look at how the equivalent room is laid out and furnished, measuring the major items in it, the spaces around it, and transferring those dimensions outside.

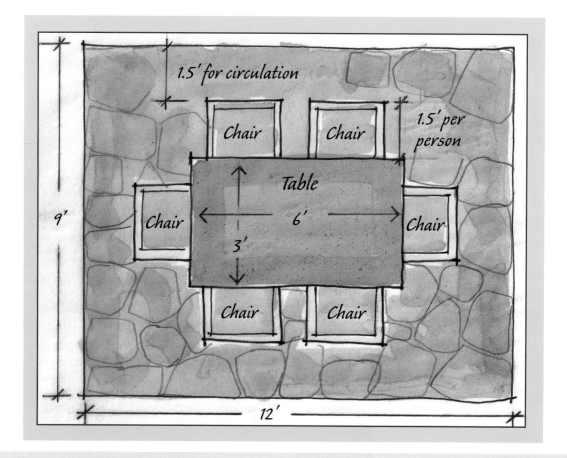

Rule of thumb for dining areas: Take the dimensions of the table you'll use (visit a patio shop to find the right size dining set to suit your needs), and add three feet around the table on all sides. That gives you 18" for a chair with a seated person, and another 18" to push the chair back or for someone to walk behind it. A typical rectangular table for six people measures approximately 5 feet by 3 feet. So your minimum level paved area needs to be at least 12 feet x 9 feet. Use this same practical approach to determine the practical size for any useable active space: function should take precedence over form.

Note: Play equipment needs lots of extra space for safety surfacing such as shredded rubber tires, soft sand, wood chips, or pea gravel, so ask for safety guidelines at the place of purchase.

Privacy

I have a neighbor with big picture windows in the front room and no drapes. On my evening dog walks with Biff the Wonder Spaniel, I feel like I'm at an off-off-Broadway play, voyeuristically peering into their mysterious lives. If you're comfortable living your life on display, fine, but if you'd like to avoid having your daily doings the subject of someone else's Facebook posts, allow space in your design for screening plants or a fence. As you list your outdoor rooms, jot down whether you'll want to increase your "invisibility."

Space for Stuff

Raise your hand if you have way too much storage space and not nearly enough crap. Didn't think so. Enjoyable outdoor living calls for places to conveniently store bench cushions, lawn games, gnome-washing gear, and other stuff. The simplest solution is an out-of-sight storage shed or two, but in small yards, that might not be possible. Integrate your storage needs in a built-in bench with a hinged seat. Find a shed you'll enjoy looking at, or use its walls to camouflage it with a beautiful vertical succulent garden.

Important, But Not So Sexy: the supporting players

Good yards need good infrastructure and this is the point in the planning phase to consider the things that make your yard tick. While you're dreaming your outdoor living dreams, make a list of the supporting elements that let the room do its job. Fountains, irrigation systems and veggie gardens need convenient access to water; pumps, appliances and lighting need electricity; fire pits need

natural gas. Now is the time to add those necessities to your list, so you don't have a "How did I forget about that?" moment, and find yourself jackhammering your brand new patio – and depleting your college fund in the process. (I'll give you lots of tips about this stuff in Part 3, which is all about the structural part of your yard, the hardscape.)

Yards for People with Disabilities...and for Aging Boomers

Don't look now, but while reading this sentence, you and I and a whole lot of people got older. My recognition of that universal truth hit on a recent birthday, realizing I could finally buy a *blah* cup of fast-food coffee at a discount if I said "senior."

The good news is that, as a nation, we're living longer and staying active decades beyond recent generations. That means we can enjoy our gardens into our golden years – reason enough to design them for safety, comfort, and utility from the start. It doesn't matter whether we're as strong and supple as in our college years, or dealing with the inevitable restrictions of aging minds and bodies – a good yard is an enabling yard. A bad yard ignores the fact that not everyone is created equal.

The reality is that one in five people will face a temporary or permanent disability in their lifetime. So why not design our yards to accommodate all abilities?

A lot of work has been done in the last few decades to design barrier-free gardens for people with disabilities, and much of that work can be used to add value to yards for everyone. Known as Universal Design Principles, they have been applied primarily to architecture, yet most of the concepts apply equally well outdoors.

Most of the ideas I'm presenting fit seamlessly into any style garden. They can provide benefits even for the twenty-something woman who finds herself on crutches after winter break. These are not detailed solutions, but a broad list of issues to consider. Some will apply to your project and some might not, but as long as you're in design mode, you might as well throw some of these concepts into the mix.

Safety First

A landscape architect's primary responsibility is designing spaces that are safe for users and it should be your top concern as well. Many safety requirements are dictated by building codes. These are imposed by city, county, state/province, and federal agencies. Typical codes include plumbing, electrical, grading, and structural stability.

In addition to these codes, I want to offer some points to consider as your design progresses. (For more information, see Resources at the back of the book.)

- Slip-resistant surfaces with good traction (no moss), smooth, firm stepping-stones (no puddles) increase safe movement.
- Thorny plants, overhanging branches, sharp edges, unfinished metal and splinter-prone wood should be avoided at all costs.
- Level walkways or gentle slopes improve mobility and give adequate maneuverability room for scooters and walkers.
- Handrails at stairs and guardrails at elevation changes reduce the chance of falls.
- Strong visual contrast at steps and along path edges, as well as good lighting, helps those with visual impairments
- Sitting areas in sun and shade provide places to rest in different types of weather. Benches with backrests give support, and armrests assist when arising. Allow space for a wheelchair near benches.
- Gate openers, hose bibs and other hardware should be friendly to those with arthritic hands and/or low vision.
- Space heaters or a fire pit extend the garden's useable hours.
- Container gardens, edibles in raised beds, pulleys for hanging plants and vertical garden trellises bring plants off the ground, making gardening fun for people who have trouble bending.

Universal design creates an environment that welcomes and supports by making things comfortable and convenient for as many different people at as many stages of life as possible.

It doesn't have to increase the cost of the finished product if you include universal design concepts at this early stage. The value it adds will be appreciated for years to come.

CHAPTER 4

brainstorming your space planning

I think I've got it!

Here's your chance to try out different design scenarios before you move a teaspoon of soil.

In my practice, I've seen dozens of potentially wonderful gardens messed up by a haphazard, "what should we do this weekend" approach to space planning. If you were designing a new house or planning a major remodel, you'd think long and hard about the floor plan – the bone structure that supports your lifestyle – before anything else. The same approach to the interior applies when we step beyond the walls and contemplate our life outdoors.

Let's review what we've done so far:

- The site analysis zoomed in on your yard's opportunities and constraints.
- The needs assessment revealed your practical as well as aesthetic needs.
- Then, you sharpened your focus by conjuring up concept statements for your outdoor rooms.

Okay, it's time now to tap into your freewheeling right brain and ask your judgmental, self-critical lobe to go have a beer. It's time for bubble diagrams!

bubbling with options

In a nutshell, bubble diagramming is brainstorming with squiggles. It's a quick, free way to generate different layouts for your yard, using a simple graphic vocabulary. Not confident about your artistic skills? Still traumatized by the D you received in finger-painting class? You don't have to be Claude Monet to do this, and I promise, this will be fun and worth your time.

The drawings on the following pages show the development of two few bubble diagrams for the same front yard. There are four symbols used to draw a bubble diagram:

An oval or circle that represents an outdoor use area, i.e., **dining patio, fire pit, spa, etc.**

A squiggle that shows where you need screening, i.e., **anything, built or grown, that interrupts a view or breaks up a space.**

A double-headed arrow, **indicating the path system**

A big ol' asterisk that represents a focal point – **that cool thing that draws the eye, like a fountain or spectacular plant.**

If you're going to put this on paper (and I strongly recommend you do), grab these supplies from your Home Design Studio (Appendix B):

- An outline sketch of your yard drawn on graph paper
- Tracing paper to lay over the sketch (available at office supply stores)
- Tape to hold down the paper (the kind you can lift off, like painter's tape)
- Something to draw with

Tape the outline sketch to a table or poster board, then overlay it with a sheet of tracing paper, taped over the original. This way, you can sketch lots of bubble diagrams without marring your base sheet.

Rules & Tips: In brainstorming, anything goes. You can draw the four elements in any order. Most people start with trying out the outdoor rooms in different locations, then connecting them with paths, adding screening where necessary – then spicing the yard up with eye candy.

But let's say you already have a key back yard focal point you can see from the front door all the way through the living room window – a spectacular flowering tree, maybe – then you might want to start with that and let the design flow from there. The important thing is to work quickly, generate a lot of variations, and make your critical judgments later. Better yet, set aside some bubbling time for after your nightly bubble bath, or after dinner, when the second glass of Pinot kicks in.

Brainstorming a problem situation: In the examples you are about to see, the front door is at the end of a straight, narrow path connected to the driveway, and framed by the garage wall and a big post. It's expedient, it works, but it lacks charm.

I'd rather have guests arrive through the front garden, so I try a few configurations that ignore the path that's there. Then I knock out a few schemes where I keep the existing walkway. At 10 minutes per sketch – if it takes longer, you're thinking too much – this is a quick way to ask "what if...?"

If your imagination needs a jump-start, try this technique: Untape the drawing, rotate the base sheet 180 degrees, and start sketching again. I can't explain why, but you'll find that your design point of view has changed radically. Instead of feeling like you're across the street looking at your house, now you're inside looking out on your front yard. I guarantee you'll see fresh possibilities.

Choosing Your Best Bubble Diagram

After you've drawn as many variations as you can, draw two columns somewhere on each paper and label them Good and Bad. Under each heading, jot down a few words about what you like from that design and what you don't. For example, in the Good column, you write "interesting path, strong focal point location." And in the Bad column, "not enough privacy, impractical for wheeling trash cans." After analyzing each bubble diagram this way, you'll find a clear favorite, or you can re-sketch a composite solution that melds the best of each bubble diagram.

Save all versions, but mark your favorite. We'll be coming back to this milestone in your design later on.

If it feels like you've done a lot of heavy lifting and exhausted a big batch of brain cells, congratulations! You've accomplished a lot and probably have come away with a fresh perspective regarding your yard. Sorting through all the information you've collected and turning into something that serves your needs is no small task.

GOOD	BAD
PRIVACY	TOO SHADY
SPA NEAR BEDROOM	FOCAL POINT

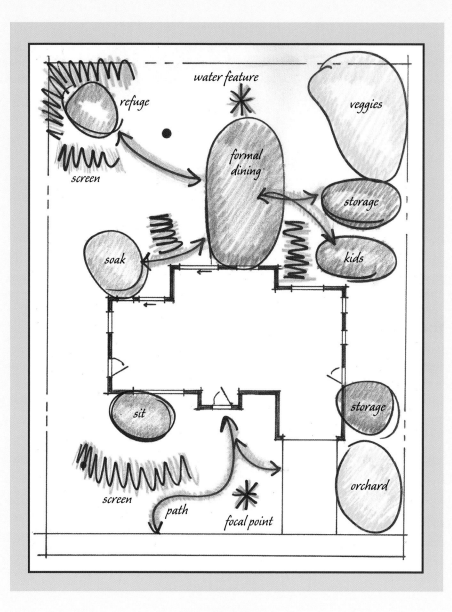

Concept #1

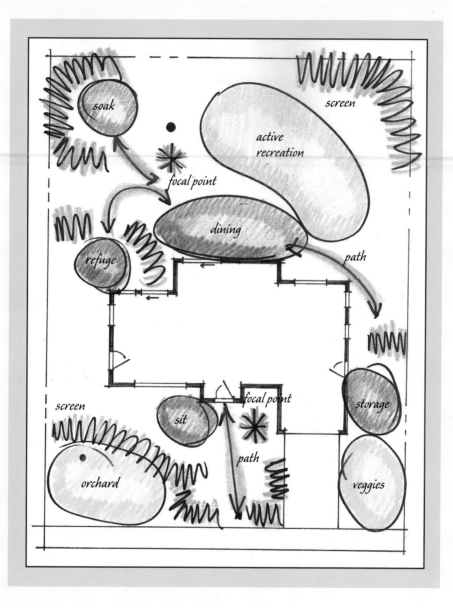

Concept #2

PART 2

aesthetics

Get your senses involved

By now you've recalibrated the pre-frontal neo-cortical design lobe of your brain. (There's no such thing.) You're thinking deep and hard about the practical side of designing a landscape that really meets your needs. But it's not enough to have a yard that simply does its job. A dream garden needs to tickle your senses and make you feel alive.

My objective in this section is to fine-tune your powers of observation by revealing the many attributes that plants and other elements display. We'll concentrate on a few of the major characteristics so you'll be able to dissect the gardens you enjoy and learn from them.

CHAPTER 5

the "why" of personal taste

Honing in on your own

*Y*ou know beauty (and ugly) when you see it, but can you put your finger on why some gardens get your endorphins flowing while others trigger your gag reflex? I'd love to write a philosophical treatise on the nature of beauty, but I'm not that smart. Instead, I'll save both of us some time by giving you permission to be inspired by, and then borrow from, the best.

Don't worry about stealing someone else's garden – you couldn't if you wanted to. Even on side-by-side parcels, the variations in growing conditions, lot layout, and your personal taste make rubber-stamp duplication unlikely. But you can use gardens you're attracted to as the jumping-off point for creating a garden that's uniquely you. (Later, in the Plagiarism chapter, I'll show you specific techniques for how to draw inspiration from other people's gardens.)

To design a yard you'll love, you need to do three things:

1. Train yourself to recognize gardens you find to be beautiful and appropriate for your home. This step takes conscious self-awareness and analysis. It helps you narrow the possibilities and clarify your style preference.
2. Figure out why you like them. When you can explain, "I like this because…" you'll discover the features you're attracted to so you can adapt them for your own needs.
3. Use those gardens as a starting point for your creation. When you can understand what's going on in the designs you like, you run a much higher chance of creating something like those gardens for yourself.

For those of you who have trouble dissecting and learning from gardens you like, this second part of the book will build your powers of observation and give you the vocabulary you'll need to clearly identify your personal preferences and move forward. Once you do that, your self-confidence as a designer will soar.

I Have Opinions

As a kid, the only thing I knew about gardens was that my mom would break out in a rash if she touched ivy. As fate would have it, an endless green mat of this devil's spawn surrounded our suburban Los Angeles front yard. On the plus side, removing this scourge gave my big brother, David, and me a chance to brandish picks and machetes. I'm happy to report that, between us, we still have an adequate number of digits to get through life.

By my twenties, I was a professional drummer living in Los Angeles, and through a series of inexplicable coincidences, I found my gateway drug to horticulture: Bonsai – the exquisite Japanese art that distills the power and beauty of nature into 3-D, palm-size, living sculpture. Practicing bonsai opened the gate to Japanese gardens, which draw on nature as a starting point for interpreting the world around us, while taming and refining it for our enjoyment and contemplation.

Bonsai – my gateway to horticulture

We're all different. Perhaps your attraction to grand floral displays was instilled as a kid when you helped with your aunt's perennial border; or maybe your love of formal, architecturally structured gardens was sparked by a visit to an English estate with classic topiary and garden ornaments. As a designer, I fully appreciate the thought, artistry, and care that go into grand gardens. But frankly, they just don't make my pulse pound.

The gardens I design, and the ones I enjoy looking at in books, are those where plants still look like plants, for the most part left unmolested to express their natural form and inherent beauty. Gardens don't have to be exact recreations of wilderness – I love contemporary designs, bold floral displays and playfulness, too. But I need to see a connection between natural processes and a created garden.

The gardens that really get my thong in a twist are the ones where plants are treated like objects to be subdued, regardless of their inherent, natural form. You see this type of adversarial gardening everywhere, where power tools are summoned to force the will of the wielder upon the hapless plants. I have zero tolerance for the mow-and-blow services, with their mindless, gotta-look-busy-for-the-owner shear-ing of plants, hacked to imitate shipping containers, flying saucers, and meatballs.

That's not to say there isn't a place in some gardens for formal shaping of plants, but I think there needs to be a conscious, aesthetically-driven thought process that leads to the decision ("I'll shape that dwarf holly into a sphere to contrast the visual chaos of the foxgloves around it"). And that design decision needs to be tempered by thinking of the maintenance impact years into the future, to make sure you're willing to enter into a long-term relationship with your shrubbery.

Yes, I have some strong opinions about what makes a garden beautiful, useful and sustainable. I figured I'd be up front about it so you'll know where the heat comes from.

Plants allowed to achieve natural form

Bougainvillea imitating awnings – not natural

You and Monet: Finding the Art in Garden Design

If someone visiting your yard asks, "Did you do that on purpose?" your yard needs help. There are a lot of reasons why your yard might look like a train derailment. Often, it results from a series of impulsive I-wonder-what's-new-at-the-nursery decisions, replayed over many years. I'm not saying you need to completely stifle your spontaneity, but you're more likely to make well-considered design decisions if you understand the fundamentals of visual design and apply them to your choices.

The same principles that guide fine artists, graphic designers, and architects apply to landscape design. In a nutshell, you have a nearly limitless palette of elements you hope to combine into a coherent, attractive composition. Graphic designers use typefaces, paper, images and white space to communicate their message. In the yard, your palette includes the dirt under your feet, plants, paving materials, pottery, wood, water, views, etc. Regardless of the ingredients you use, or the purpose of the finished product, you'll be happier with the results if you increase your command of basic design principles.

In this next chapter, I'm introducing the fundamentals of visual design that I think you'll find useful. Later, we'll apply these concepts and vocabulary to help you analyze the gardens you like, so you can create the garden of your dreams.

CHAPTER 6

key aesthetic elements in your design

*I*n a garden, you have the opportunity to exploit the visual characteristics of a broad range of design elements.

The Space-to-Stuff Balance

Unless you're contemplating annexation of your neighbors' properties, every yard has a finite volume of space to work within. When you look at a garden, the first thing I want you to notice is how much empty space there is and how much of the garden is filled with plants and furnishings.

Space includes the patio, lawn, paths – anywhere you can move around without smashing your shins or getting stuck. Everything else is stuff. In a Zen garden, a few well-chosen, dramatically arranged stones dominate an otherwise empty canvas of raked gravel. Lotsa space; not much stuff. Conversely, in a woodland garden, you might need a guide and a machete to clear enough space to stroll. On a brand new lot, it's just the house and a lot of nothing.

Stuff refers to the amenities you'll need to enjoy your yard – like tables, chairs, benches, spa. It

also includes the trees, shrubs, vines, and perennials that will bring life to your garden. Take note of this space/stuff balance in your current yard. Figure out how this principle is applied to the gardens you aspire to. Getting this fundamental concept right is crucial to meeting your aesthetic and practical goals.

Shape

Everything in a garden – spaces as well as objects – has a shape. Plants can be low and horizontal or stand up like punctuation marks. Your terrace might end up as a simple rectangle or inspired by the organic form of a ragged shoreline. And since gardens are the sum of many parts, each one comes with an opportunity and an obligation to make a conscious design decision about its form, placement and role in the big scheme.

Lines, Straight or Curving

Straight or curving, lines are the most obvious form generators in the landscape. In formal gardens, built elements and plants often conform to a grid of right angles, usually arising from the geometry of the house.

Formal gardens might also include other geometric forms, like circles, arcs, triangles, rectangles, and all manner of polygons.

Most beginning garden designers feel comfortable defaulting to formal plans, which are also easiest to lay out and build, but might be short on the whimsy or excitement you seek. But straight lines don't have to be static. Kicking your path system on a 20-degree angle from the house generates visual tension, as well as opportunities for impressive planting beds.

It's been said, "Nature abhors a straight line." If you're more inclined toward a naturalistic setting, put down your T-square, have a second beer and loosen up your elbow. When designing with curves, the simpler the better. Paths and border edges that meander like a drunken penguin distract the eye and look contrived. For inspiration, observe how natural forces smoothly carve out riverbeds, or form flowing drifts of plants.

Color

When I'm using my computer's scanner, one of my setting options says "Millions of colors." That's a bit much to comprehend, so let's look at the color wheel for a straightforward lesson in color theory basics.

The three primary colors (also called hues) are red, blue, and yellow. Mix any two primaries to produce the secondary colors, orange, green, and violet. Now we've got six. Further mixing of adjacent colors produces tertiary hues: yellow-green, orange-red, etc., for an even dozen.

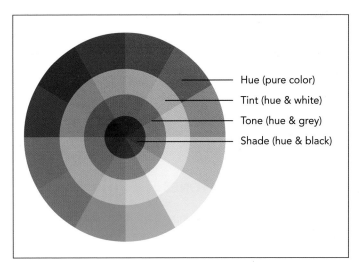

Hue (pure color)
Tint (hue & white)
Tone (hue & grey)
Shade (hue & black)

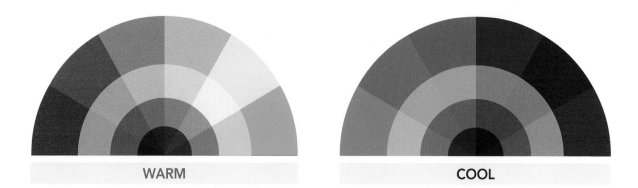

WARM   **COOL**

Warm colors – yellow-green through orange to red-violet – are associated with daylight, and appear to advance toward the viewer. Their ability to arouse and stimulate makes them valuable for a showy visual splash from a distance, or when used to make small spaces sparkle. *Cool colors* – violet through blue to green – appear to recede, giving them less impact from a distance, but they make a good choice for spaces where you want to chill out.

Your yard's overall color scheme can include vignettes using contrasting combos (pairing colors from opposite poles of the wheel), as well as analogous schemes, using harmonious colors close to each other on the wheel. More on this later.

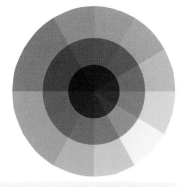

TINTS, SHADES AND TONES

Once you have a handle on these basic color concepts, explore the tints, tones and shades of these basic hues to add variety to your palette. Follow me back to kindergarten finger-painting class for a color refresher. The teacher comes by with her cart and plops down a blob of red paint on your paper, followed by a white chaser. An instant later, you're shmooshing them together, when, Eureka!!! You've created PINK!!! Pink is what's known as the tint of red. Similarly, salmon is the tint of orange; lavender comes from mixing violet with white. Mix white with any hue and you get its tint. Still with me? Combine a bit of white and black to make grey, then add that to the hue. The effect will make the color subtler, like looking at it through a light haze.

Soon the teacher returns, dropping a wicked dollop of black on your paper, and when you've mixed that with your red, you're rewarded with maroon, the shade of red. Black and yellow? Gold. Black and green? Think pine forest.

Playing with Color in Your Plant Selections

How do we apply these tint and shade concepts to picking out plants for your yard? What about leaving out the red and pairing up the two extremes, pink and maroon? Leaving out the hue yields stronger contrast.

But by using two colors derived from the same source, you know they'll play nicely together. (More about harmony and contrast in Chapter 12) Depending on how much we blend, tint, and shade the three primary colors, it's easy to see how we can get to a million in no time.

Recognizing the nominal color of a plant is necessary for making beautiful color schemes, but there's another dimension that influences how colors appear in the garden. It's what artists call *chroma*. You can also think of this trait as *saturation*, or *intensity*. I picture it as the difference between having the color powered by one AAA battery and having it plugged into the Hoover Dam dynamo. Another way to think about chroma is how that color would look on a clear day versus on a foggy day.

For example, if I place two contrasting plants next to each other – one blue, the other orange, and each of equal size – we'd expect the orange to dominate the scene, because the warm colors have that kind of aggressive personality. But if the orange is low intensity and the blue is firing on 12 cylinders, what we think of as the cooler color would become the dominant.

The Power of Neutral Colors

Just to complicate things, I need to include the role of neutrals, like white, ivory, silver, and gray, in this discussion. Neutrals amplify the hues placed near them, harmonize disparate colors, and add a "glow in the dark" accent as daylight fades in the garden. Because of their light-reflecting character and brightness in the landscape, used alone, they act more as warm colors than cool.

Organizing the Elements for Balance, Scale & Proportion

To analyze and learn from the gardens you like, you'll need a few more tools to work with. Look at what's going on in the gardens in this section and use these concepts to better understand the designs you like and those you'd cross the street to avoid.

Balance (the teeter-totter effect)

Achieving formal, or symmetrical, balance is pretty straightforward:

- Draw an imaginary line through the center of a space.
- Arrange pairs of matching elements equidistant from the axis.
- Done!

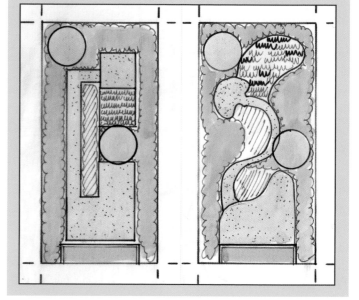

Balance can be achieved formally or informally

This approach is simple and logical, provided you have a vantage point where you can appreciate the balance, and a space you can divide in half. Some homes and sites are well suited to this approach, especially European-influenced architecture.

If you like the idea of a well-balanced garden based on an underlying geometry, but don't want it to be too rigid, consider starting with the same strong axis, but shift one or two elements off the line for a more dynamic layout. This loosening of plan will maintain a sense of balance, but without the perfect mirror image.

However, in a yard with slopes, bumps, and irregular topography, imposing a formal, geometric layout onto undulating ground will look forced. The more natural the landform, the greater the need to use an informal, or asymmetrical, composition. Remember the discussion about space and stuff in the last chapter?

Here's where those ideas come into play. Picture a playground teeter-totter with identical twins sitting on each end. That's formal balance. When the kids are done bouncing around, Dad shows up, plunks himself down on one side and tells the kids to try to raise him off the ground. Dad's been hitting the Twinkies pretty hard, so the twins round up a half-dozen friends, pile onto the other side, the teeter-totter starts to groan, then up goes Dad. That's asymmetrical balance.

If you think of plants and objects in the garden as having "visual weight" you'll see where this is going. A 20-foot tall tree with dark, dense foliage in one corner of the yard will look heavy compared to a small clump of wispy ornamental grass on the other side. To visually balance the composition, it might take a few more clumps of grass, plus a grouping of medium shrubs to keep the tree from overpowering the composition.

Scale and Proportion

In a garden, no element exists independent of the others. Like a well-crafted story, each plays a part, whether a supporting role or as a lead character. Along with deciding what to add and what to leave out of your yard, it's just as important to consider how each piece contributes to the whole.

That's where scale and proportion come in.

Scale refers to the overall size of something: Think Goldilocks and the Three Bears' chairs. For example, visit your local garden center and you'll find water features ranging from table-top bubblers to birdbaths to grand tiered fountains. Similarly, plants can range in scale from delicate ground covers to towering oaks. Keep this in mind when selecting the ingredients for your garden.

Proportion describes one object's visual relationship with another. A small cottage can appear larger surrounded with low growing, fine textured plants, just as a large house appears smaller than it actually is when flanked by massive oak trees. A simple picket fence would look just right surrounding the cottage, while a stone balustrade could hold its own with the big house.

Proportion can be thought of as a ratio, or pie chart.

Here's an example of proportion in developing a color scheme: Say you choose to work with pastels – tints of lavender and pink, and adding some silvery foliage. But how much of each to use? 90% lavender with speckles of pink and silver will have a very different appearance than using equal parts of each.

Applying the Principles of Scale and Proportion to Different-Size Spaces

In small gardens, you'll want to start with uncomplicated patterns, fine textured foliage, a muted floral color scheme, intimate furnishings, and small objects. The objective is to have the proportions of each element complement, not overwhelm, the space.

Larger spaces benefit from darker colors in canopy, lighter below, bold patterns, and bolder textures. If the overall garden feels like a big, empty warehouse, consider subdividing the overall space into a series of rooms, or filling them with warm colors and large-scale artwork. Tables, chairs, and other furnishing with a little more bulk to them will help to tame the space and bring it into balance.

The tricky thing is that, unlike your front room, the proportions of a garden change over time. Plants grow, causing spaces to shrink. In other parts of the garden, where maturing trees cast shade on plants that need more sun, gaps might occur, leading to a thinning of the understory. These are part of the evolution of a garden – remembering that a garden isn't a product; it's a process.

Three Schematic Garden Plans: Same Design Elements, Three Different Styles

I've thrown a lot at you so far in these pages. But it's all been so that we can wrap our arms around the basic aspects of good design. You've used the analysis process to determine what you have to work with and where you want to go. And the bubble diagram exercise resulted in a configuration of rooms, paths, screening and focal points.

Now I'd like to show you how the same set of elements can be expressed in several different ways, depending on your personal taste preferences. Your goal is a schematic plan that establishes the actual forms the built elements of the garden will take, drawn to scale. By determining how much space the built elements will consume, you'll know exactly what's left for your plants. Once that's done, it's a matter of picking out the final construction materials and finishes.

There are many variations on these themes, depending on how much space you have to work with and per-sonal preference. You might even combine a few, for instance, using a formal grid adjacent to the house and gradually softening the lines as the visual influence of the house lessens.

Once you've decided on the form your garden will take, you'll be ready to tackle the nuts and bolts details that will result in a garden that blends your aesthetic desires with the practical, day-to-day demands of gracious outdoor living.

Here, I've drawn three different-but-the-same gardens, all based on the same bubble diagram, but each expressed in a different style. This is by no means an exhaustive exploration of all the possibilities, but demonstrates how personal taste and style can influence the finished dream garden.

For those who've been reading along and doing the suggested drawings, study the process I'm describing and try your hand at further refining your schematic plan. Here we go…

Informal, Naturalistic Style

This approach has a casual feeling using "organic," flowing forms you might find in nature. It can be used with almost any style of architecture.

Features:

- flowing lines
- asymmetrical balance
- irregular massing of plants
- focal point offset

Formal Grid

This treatment plays off the proportions of the house and has a more stationary feeling. Try this layout with classic architectural styles.

Features:

- parallel and perpendicular lines
- regular geometric forms and arcs
- symmetrical balance
- static planting beds

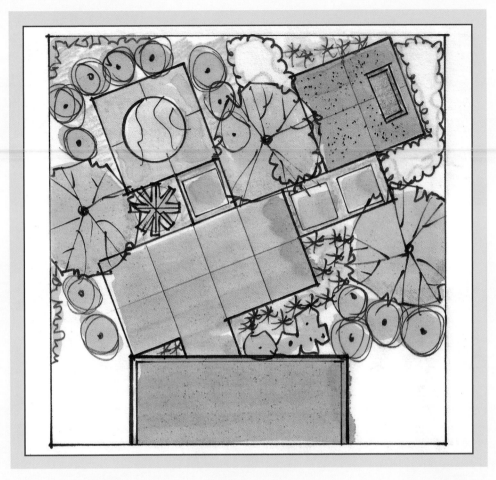

Skewed/Angular Grid

This is a more playful, "artsy" direction, using the grid approach, but kicking it off kilter. It adds a feeling of dynamism and is well suited to contemporary forms of architecture.

Features:

- dynamic use of space
- corner beds have more depth
- plants follow grid but leap across edges

CHAPTER 7

a garden that evolves with the seasons

How to think about a year-round garden

J live and work in Santa Barbara, an enviable subtropical paradise where some clients expect their gardens to perform at full throttle all the time. As I prepare a preliminary plant list for them to consider, I brace myself because I know they'll insist that none of the plants ever lose their leaves, or have to be cut back from time to time. I find this shortsighted. If you want a static garden, frozen in time 365 days a year, I say hire a Hollywood set designer, paint a convincing backdrop and staple some silk flowers on it.

Live in a cold climate? I know that spring is the season you gardeners lust for. All the Easter egg colors come into bloom and gawky, skeletal shrubs begin to bush out. But what if, instead of focusing your attention on this much-anticipated though short-lived event, you designed your garden for year-round enjoyment?

Surprising with Mass and Space

There's a natural cycle in the cosmos and we need to embrace it in the garden. And I'm not just talking about fall color or crocus popping their sweet pink buds through the snow. Entire volumes of space can be transformed when billowing ornamental grasses like Miscanthus – achieving the proportions of a small haystack – are cut to the ground in late fall, opening up lines of sight to parts of the garden hidden since mid-summer. Not taking "no" for an answer, the plant starts up again and the garden becomes more intimate and mysterious. I delight in gardens that ebb and flow, displaying multiple personalities throughout the year.

Playing with Light and Shade

As seasons change, so do our living patterns. I've shared my view that the more we design our gardens as outdoor rooms, the more we get back for our effort. The same goes for creating spaces that give us a front seat to seasonal changes. When you develop your site plan it's logical to locate your cozy reading nook to take advantage of the cool shade (and luscious fruit) of a mulberry tree in summer. Think a little deeper to also make it a welcoming winter garden room oriented to catch toasty morning light, where you can watch a blue bird gleaning the last seeds from your collapsing sunflower.

Appreciating Flowing Water: the rain garden

Where summer rains are commonplace, integrate storm water run-off solutions that invite beauty, sound and movement to the garden. Aside from the environmental benefits – filtering out pollutants, slowing and absorbing water that would otherwise go down the gutter, replenishing groundwater basins – water that flows through the garden has decorative potential. Rain gardens can create magic. Even in arid climates, a downpour can bring a dry arroyo to life and fill the air with the raspy music of croaking frogs.

Planning Seasonal Color Schemes

Although it's possible to maintain the same color scheme throughout the growing seasons, I think a it's a lot more fun to design a garden that evolves with the seasons.

Spring is when the garden hits the reset button. Days can be a mixed bag of sunshine, cold blasts, showers and clouds. The garden eases back into action, the perfect stage for soft pastel colors like sky blue, buttery yellow, muted mauve, baby-cheek pink. Include early blooming shrubs like witch hazel, camellias, forsythia and magnolia in your beds. Work annuals and perennials in complementary colors into the mix, and if you plan ahead, the bulbs you planted before the fall temperatures dropped will start putting on a show.

Summer color schemes should warm up as the sun's intensity increases. The hours of daylight increase and we spend more time in our yards enjoying the longer days and inviting nights. This is when the garden is ready for its close-up. When I design a bed that has to dazzle from a distance, I reach for reds, oranges or yellows. These hues bring energy, good cheer, feelings of abundance, even sensuality. They seem to holler, "Look over here!"

Fall brings another opportunity to switch up the look of your garden. If you've worked ornamental grasses into your scheme, watch them turn tawny shades of straw. In colder climates, summer green has receded from the leaves, exposing the warm color pigments that remain.

Ignore hot fall color at your peril; nothing worse than having a softly pastel container arrangement thrown off by brilliant lava-red leaves of a burning bush *(Euonymus alata)*.

Of course, in most gardening areas, deciduous plants are unavoidable. In keeping with my design philosophy that gardens be a reflection of the natural environment, it makes sense to accept, embrace, and take advantage of the changes that occur throughout the year.

Winter, where I live, just means putting on a pair of socks with my flip flops. But if you keep a snow blower handy in your garage, this is for you. Where snow covers the ground for much of the winter season, there's not much you can do about floral color, so build your garden around evergreen plants that retain their form, while also paying attention to variations in foliage color. Conifers can range from the deepest greens (most pines and junipers) to silvery-blue (Colorado blue spruce) tints. When skies are dreary there's nothing like a burst of golden-green (Lawson cypress 'Stardust') to create interest. Some deciduous trees and shrubs sport colorful bare branches, like the fiery red-twig dogwood. And don't overlook the contribution of your furnishings and garden ornaments to overcome a gray day.

CHAPTER 8

the sensual garden

Sound, Scent, Touch, Movement, Memory

Whether you subscribe to the Garden of Eden scenario or that we arose from the primordial ooze, clearly, we are creatures of nature. For millennia, we relied on our wits and our senses for survival. But our modern lives have, unfortunately, allowed us to get through the day using only a fraction of our senses: pressing the mute button when a commercial comes on, listening for the "bing" that tells us a fresh e-mail has arrived, noticing that the morning application of armpit armor has expired.

What if your garden became a place where you could engage your senses to enrich your daily life? My job is to show you the greater potential of your outdoor spaces where you can't wait to spend your free time. (One alternative would be enlarging a picture of a garden from your favorite calendar and plugging in one of those lilac-scented oil gizmos and comfortably staying in the house.) Just like sex, our senses serve a practical purpose, but that doesn't mean we can't have some fun with them, too.

With a little imagination and planning, your yard will become a garden of earthly delights.

Let's take a quick tour around your head. We've been over nearly everything you can do in the garden for your eyes: the concepts of color, harmony, contrast, and the rest. It's time to do something for the other senses.

Exercise Your Ears

If you're fortunate enough to live away from the continuous drone of civilization, you're already clued in on how your sense of hearing comes into play when you're in the yard. I heard my first cicadas a few years ago while visiting Raleigh, North Carolina. Once I realized I wasn't on a sci-fi movie set, I was struck by how

the sound of insects connected me to the world just beyond the familiarity of my host's backyard. (Of course, the next sound that connected to nature was the whine of a mosquito, followed by the smack of my hand on my ear.)

You can bring pleasant sounds to your garden by introducing plants that attract local songbirds. And you don't need George Frideric Handel to express water music around your terrace. Dramatic waterfalls roar, while gently flowing streams whoosh over rocks.

If you live in a breezy area and choose your plants with sound in mind, you can enjoy the rustle of leaves in a willow tree, the whisper of wind through tall grasses, or the percussive clatter of bamboo. Grow and dry gourds with your kids for a pair of DIY maracas. If you're really ambitious and can simulate the climate of Sri Lanka, try your hand at growing ebony *(Diospyros ebenum)* and make your own clarinet.

Wind chimes come in a range of sizes and pitches, from throaty baritones to delicate tinkling. Or you can be lazy, install a few Bose speakers under the eaves and pipe the garden full of your favorite Serbo-Croatian mariachi hits.

Nudge Your Nose

It goes without saying (then why am I saying it?) that there are some dazzlingly lovely floral scents we can incorporate into the garden, starting with roses for your noses. That's a start, but what about aromatic foliage

to tickle your nostrils? (Just a second; I feel a sneeze coming on.) I have a client who asked for lemon-scented thyme between stepping stones. It makes a garden walk seem like a spa treatment. Place chocolate-mint scented geranium in patio pots where you can brush them with your hand – it's almost like having dessert.

Newly mowed grass triggers my memories of childhood, freshly turned soil triggers a primal response, and I can't think of a more gratifying smell than well-seasoned compost. And let's not forget the Pavlovian response some folks get when a big fat steak sizzles on the grill.

A word of caution: As with perfume, a little bit of flora fragrance goes a long way. Too many plants going off at once can be an olfactory overload. And some people are very sensitive to certain fragrances, triggering asthma-like symptoms, so do your homework and be prepared to move a few plants around, and proceed with caution.

Feel Me, Touch Me

Fuzzy lamb's ear foliage reminds you of your plush childhood cuddly toy. An overflowing urn beckons you to plunge your hand in its cool water. The spongy bark of a cork oak submits to your fingernail. When breezes blow, you sense the moving air in your hair and on your skin.

I find that the sense of touch tends to be overlooked in gardens, but it's our primary connection to our world. I try to exploit it every chance I get.

Movement

Yes, pictures of gardens are lovely to look at. But real gardens are intended to be lived in, moved through. Your choice of path material affects movement and how you experience space. Sinuous gravel paths shift and crunch, slowing you down; sensible, straight concrete walkways make rolling the trash to the curb almost enjoyable. Design a space for pleasurable movement, where you can practice tai-chi or watch (join?) your kids as they dance and roll around.

Movement enlivens the garden when hummers zip between honeysuckle blossoms and prairie grasses, palm trees, willows and bamboo submit to a stiff gust.

A garden isn't only three-dimensional – their fourth dimension is time. If you have the space, design a series of different garden tableaus and thread them along a path where you can experience them in succession.

Memory Lane

Find something in your life that brings back happy memories and give it a special home in your garden.

While on their second honeymoon in Monterey, California, two clients of mine had bought a gigantic cast iron colander-like artifact – rusted and heavy as a small VW. When we met, it had been stashed behind the garage for years, serving as a habitat for spiders. The antique dealer said it had been used on Cannery Row to plunge hundreds of crabs at a time into boiling water. We resurrected it as the focal point of the couple's back yard, visible from three rooms in the house and brimming with seasonal flowers year-round.

PART 3

hardscape

If it isn't green, it's hardscape

Before we get to the really fun stuff – designing the plantings – it's important to nail down the other elements of your dream garden. I'm talking about the permanent or semi-permanent things, like the plumbing and electrical, the concrete and stone and wood, and all the other furnishings that set the stage for outdoor living.

Once these parts are in place, it's unlikely you'll be enthusiastic about changing them. So it's better to think them through now rather than rent a jackhammer in a few years when you finally come to the realization that, "I probably shoulda…" There are a lot of puzzle pieces to integrate. I'll walk you through the thought process a professional designer uses, so you don't miss some critical details.

This section will also help you sort out whether to follow your do-it-yourself instincts or bring in professional help during the design and/or construction phases.

Important note: In Appendix C, I provide a description of the various kinds of services and professionals that are available to you, should you need them.

CHAPTER 9

infrastructure and systems

Plumbing, Electricity, Gas, Drainage

*B*efore a shovelful of soil gets moved, think ahead to all the underground utilities and services you'll be grateful for once your garden is finished.

You'll never see a picture of a sewer cleanout or water pressure regulator on the cover of Architectural Digest. That's not an image that makes magazines fly off the shelves. But one day you'll be very happy that your architect included them in his plans. The same goes for garden infrastructure. First up: plumbing.

Plumbing

Irrigation systems, cooking island sinks, cascading waterfalls, outdoor showers and hose bibs need to be properly sized and efficiently located around the garden. Just because you've got a good eye for combining plants and picking lovely garden ornaments doesn't necessarily mean you've got what it takes to be a hydraulic engineer. This is one place where even I know to pick up the phone and call an irrigation consultant. But if you've got a knack for this sort of thing, have at it. Most communities have an irrigation equipment supplier that sells to the trade and to homeowners, and they'll be happy to coach you.

Electricity

Although I'm not an advocate of lighting up gardens like a Broadway stage (light pollution of the night sky is one of the regrettable consequences of city living), energy-efficient, low-voltage lighting systems can add charm, increase safety and extend outdoor living time. The good news is that most of these systems simply

plug into a wall socket, using a built-in transformer to step down the charge from the dangerous 120-volt household current to a safe 12 volts. The wires leading from the transformer/controller to the fixture can either sit on the surface – snake them through ground covers or under mulch – or be concealed in shallow trenches. Be sure to subtly mark where they are, so you don't accidentally put them out of commission with a pointy tool.

But if there is not a convenient outlet where you need it, you'll want to hire an electrical contractor to install one. If there's water nearby, whether from sprinklers or because you're using the outlet for a fountain or pond, hire a licensed electrical contractor to install a ground-fault circuit interrupter (GFCI or GFI) outlet, to prevent getting shocked. This is not a do-it-yourself project! And since the conduits that house these 120-volt wires need to be buried, include this instillation early in your work.

Gas

If toasting gooey, drippy s'mores or gabbing with guests around an open flame are on your list of must-have indulgences, include natural gas or liquefied petroleum (LP) in your plans. Though they don't give you the woodsy aroma of a log campfire, the convenience of one-touch ignition and not having to dispose of ash might sway your decision. As with electricity, gas lines should be set up by a trained expert.

Drainage

If I had my druthers, I'd never send precious rainwater into a pipe and then hurry it to the gutter. In our increasingly impervious world of roofs, driveways and patios, rainwater passes over these surfaces, picking up sediment and other particles, nutrients, pathogens and chemicals that cause pollution. To make matters worse, escaping stormwater is concentrated into channels and other drainages, where it can easily increase in force, scouring and destabilizing banks. If you're thinking, "It's just my little lot; what's the big deal?" consider the multiplier effect of an entire neighborhood or community ignoring these impacts.

As you plan your garden, look for opportunities to capture, filter, or at least slow the release of stormwater from your property.

Rain barrels and cisterns can store rainwater from your roof. Rain gardens – planted, shallow depressions in the ground strategically placed along the drainage route of your yard – capture run-off from your driveway or roof, filter it through foliage, and allow it to percolate back into the ground. Select permeable surfaces like brick-on-sand, gravel, or specially designed concrete lattice pavers for paths and parking areas.

If you're stuck for space to implement these strategies and you simply have to move water away from the house and off-site, you're back in the territory of engineering. There's only so much water that can flow into a catch basin and through an underground pipe at a given time. A landscape architect or civil engineer is trained to calculate drain line sizing, depth and slope, and recommend the most effective locations to place them. Better to write a check to a pro than figure out how to dry your carpeting after a deluge.

That was a quick look at the underground portions of your new garden. Let's move up into the light of day.

CHAPTER 10

anatomy of an outdoor room

Analyzing Your Needs and Materials, from Floor to Ceiling

I start every design by picturing the yard as an extension of my clients' indoor living areas. Each room of the house has a particular function: You cook and have summit meetings in the kitchen, enjoy family time and entertain in the living room. You sleep, read, and "ahem" in the bedroom.

Each room is a specialized space designed and furnished to meet specific uses. It's not likely you'd cover your kitchen with shag carpeting any more than you'd put stone tile in the kids' playroom. That same "form follows function" approach applies when you step outside. Start by considering how the space will be used, and then how it should look. When you're done mulling that over, think about the long-term maintenance impacts of your choices. Will the materials you select take care of themselves or need frequent attention? Sometimes, spending a little more on the front end turns out to be money saved over the life of your garden.

Let's work our way from the bottom up.

Floors

If you can walk on it, store something on it, or roll around on it, I call it a floor. Paths, decks, patios, overlooks, trash can storage, lawns, ground cover plantings… they're all floors.

In design-speak, the floor is considered "negative space", that is, until you place your potted plants or an Adirondack chair on it. Aside from its functional purpose, this negative space is a valuable design element, acting as visual contrast to the plants and other stuff that fills the garden – the yin and yang of your yard.

The simplest floor material is the dirt that comes with your property. Unfortunately, the problem with an all-dirt floor is, well, it's dirty, even downright muddy when wet. It's also erodible and doesn't maintain a stable, flat surface for tables, chairs and safe footing.

Solid Floor Materials: When I think of elegant outdoor rooms, stone, brick and tile come to mind – and, with a caveat, concrete.

- Stone is elemental, taking many forms – from irregular slabs of flagstone edged with dainty ground covers, to geometric shapes solidly mortared to a slab. (Sustainable tip: When shopping for stone, start with local materials to avoid the environmental impacts of shipping all that weight cross-country.)

- The color palette for brick runs from nearly black through gray, brown, red and into yellowish tints. There are endless patterns to experiment with, including traditional running bond, herringbone, basket weave, radial spokes, or whimsical layouts that look like someone pounded down one too many beers at lunch. I'm a big fan of integrating stone and brick in the same floor to further enrich the effect.

In formal situations, brick is mortared onto a solid slab of concrete. This approach ensures that the brick will not subside or shift, a critical detail under tables and chairs. For paths, the standard approach is to set the outer edges of brick in a solid concrete base, pave the inner surface with brick set on well-compacted mason's sand, then brush more sand into the joints to lock them into place. **Warning:** Where ground freezes, loosely set brick can heave, making the path uneven and possibly dangerous. And steer clear of mature trees with surface roots.

- Tile, like brick, offers a broad palette of styles ranging from crisp, contemporary forms to old world Mediterranean. Because tile is thin and unable to bear much weight on its own, it is always mortared to a solid foundation. Be careful to avoid slick surfaces, since they can become dangerously slippery when wet.

- Square foot for square foot, concrete is a smart, long-term investment. It starts off in a semi-liquid state, meaning it can assume any shape. If plain old sidewalk-gray isn't your style, concrete can be textured and colored to look like stone, seeded with pebbles, pocked with rock salt, or stained with intense pigments to create bold designs.

One problem with traditional concrete, though, is it's impermeable, so water sheds off rather than percolating into the soil where it can do some good. See "Drainage" in the previous chapter.

Loose Floor Materials: Although it might seem like a low-budget cop-out, loose materials like gravel, crushed rock, compacted shale or decomposed granite can be inexpensive yet elegant choices, especially when bordered by a richer material, like stone or brick. Advantages include permeability, low cost and ease of installation. However, these materials are more likely to be displaced, especially if water passes over them. And gritty, sandy materials are the last things you want to track onto your hardwood entryway. One of my favorite design treatments for upgrading crushed rock paths uses enriched "thresholds" and intersections of stone.

Decks: A contractor friend of mine calls wood decks "dry rot in slow motion." He's pretty spot-on. Traditional wood decks, regardless of how much waterproofing you apply each year, will eventually succumb to nature's forces (or termites). But if you've got a sloping property, need a level surface for outdoor entertaining, and want to avoid the expense and disruption of building retaining walls, it's the way to go. Since you're not likely to add onto the deck once it's built, now is the time to decide how it will be used and make space for all the furnishings you want.

To avoid the effect of weathering and decay, consider building with manufactured plastic lumber, made from recycled bottles, plastic bags and wood scraps. It comes in standard lumber sizes, connects with screws and doesn't rot.

Plants: In addition to using inert materials for your floor, there's all the living stuff. Once again, your choice should be guided by the intended use: Active recreation calls for the evenly-mowed surface of a tended lawn. Meadows, with their tussled, just-got-out-of-bed appearance, are ideal for creating a rustic feeling – and can attract a diversity of beneficial insects and other cool things for kids to discover. You can walk through them or mow romantic, sinuous paths to explore. If you don't need to wander through the space, any combination of ankle-high perennials and ground covers can provide color and an open expanse that carries the eye across the garden.

Walls

I define garden walls as any vertical mass that reaches above eye level. You can build them, grow them, or split the difference by training a vine on a trellis.

In your bubble diagram, you drew a squiggly line indicating "screening." That's one definition of a garden wall, but there are others. Let's look at a few examples of when you might want to include one of these vertical elements, and discuss the materials available.

Privacy/Screening: Whether you're hoping to hide something or prevent others from seeing into your yard, the primary goal is interrupting the line of sight. The most obvious solution along your property lines is building a solid wall (fieldstone, concrete block, stucco over a wood frame) or wood fence with no spaces between the planks.

Choose materials and finishes that suit your garden style and make sure they're durable enough to withstand the ravages of weather and ground moisture.

You can grow your privacy, too, but consider these points.

- Plants can take years to fill in, so be patient.
- Most plants won't quit growing when they reach the desired height. Prepare to give some of your weekend time away.
- Plants can suddenly die, leaving gaping holes.

It's impractical to expect a hedge to block the view from a neighbor's upstairs window, especially a multi-story apartment building. You'd be better off with a strategically placed tree with horizontal branches that block the upward view.

Intimacy: There are situations when you'd like to screen the view of one garden room from the rest of your yard, like a meditation corner or dining terrace. In these instances, you don't need the Great Wall of China towering above, since you'll be sitting down and your eye level will be only a few feet above the ground. Tall screens can make a garden room feel claustrophobic, reduce air circulation, and make it too shady. This is when an informal planting of medium-size shrubs might be the best call. You can select plants for color and fragrance, adding charm to the surroundings.

Security: It's not unneighborly to want to keep uninvited guests and critters out of your yard. In most situations, a six-foot-high wall or fence gets the job done. Dense hedges can eventually do the job, but as explained above, there's no guarantee the plants will continue to thrive years from now.

Backdrop: Don't overlook the importance of walls and screens in your overall design scheme. Every surface, built or grown, has visual characteristics that influence everything around them. Consider how a boldly colored stucco wall can boost the intensity of your planting: If your garden is bounded by tall shrubs, it's not likely you'll be able to pretend that the flaming orange flowers of a tecoma vine aren't overpowering the delicate pink blossoms of your Wildeve® David Austin rose bush.

Wind: A gentle breeze is welcome in the garden, but the gust that blows your dinner plate off the patio table? Not so much. An effective windbreak can also reduce frigid winter winds and keep snow from piling up around your home. Built windbreaks, in the form of walls and fences, can have their drawbacks, since wind will compress when it encounters a vertical surface, then spill over turbulently, making the effective calm area relatively small. Where space allows, a better strategy is to plant a progression of low, medium and then tall evergreen plants that gently lift the wind, so it rises, then continues in a laminar flow.

Ceilings

Every room in your house needs a ceiling, but that doesn't hold true for your entire garden. We welcome views of the sky and sunshine, and many of the plants we love need lots of direct rays. But sometimes it's nice to have something between you and the heavens.

As with garden floors and walls, you have the option of growing your ceiling or building something. The ceilings you select for your garden will be driven by what you want them to do.

Shade: When summer temperatures climb, folks like me turn into banana slugs, seeking the cool shade of a tree or covered patio. Depending on the style of garden you're creating, your budget, and your level of patience, your shade options could include: planting an affordable small tree and popping open a patio umbrella while it matures; stringing up a garden sail; erecting a trellis to support a vine; or building a roofed structure. If your aim is to create a cool retreat during hot weather only, opt for trees or vines that drop their leaves to let winter rays warm your bones.

Rain: Do you enjoy sitting outside while raindrops fall, but want to stay dry? That calls for a solid roof, usually an extension out from the house. But there's a downside. The permanent shade cast by this approach will make adjacent indoor rooms darker year-round, affecting not only the ambience of the space, but also raising your electricity bill from turning on the interior lights. Maybe better to opt for a gazebo in the garden?

⚹

On to the plants!

Once the built part of the landscape design is determined, you'll know how much space you have for planting. But stay nimble and keep your eraser handy; in the next section you might discover that you've short-changed yourself on planting "real estate" and decide to whittle down some of your hardscape footprint so you can get your horticulture groove on. After all, gardens are all about the plants.

PART 4

picking plants

How hard could it be?

Ever gone nuts picking out colors for a bedroom makeover? How many samples did you bring home and how many hours did it take to come up with a three-color wall-ceiling-trim combo you liked? If you're like most people, you probably suffered through analysis paralysis trying to decide whether Nimbus Gray or Montpelier is the best complement for Amethyst Shadow.

If landscaping your yard were as simple as picking out three plants with compatible colors, I'd be out of a job and we could ditch this chapter. Stick with me while I take the mystery out of designing a beautiful garden that does more than just look "purty."

CHAPTER 11

selecting plants that will love you back

The Process of Elimination

A typical back yard garden on a quarter-acre suburban lot will have anywhere from ten to forty different varieties of plants. The variables for that number range from a total lack of self-control to having a brown thumb where only the fittest survive. Here on the Left Coast, our plant bible is the Sunset Western Garden Book, boasting an encyclopedic collection of "OVER ,000 PLANTS!" For many parts of the country, the equivalent resource is the American Horticulture Society's A to Z Encyclopedia of Garden Plants. And there's the growing availability of online databases. So how is the average homeowner supposed to find a couple of useful needles in that massive haystack?

Keep in mind that developing a planting design isn't just about appearances. Remember, my fundamental design philosophy is that yards should be useful and sustainable, too. Not only that, but as you're well aware, you've got to keep the plants alive, no small trick given variations in soil compatibility, sunlight, watering, and the occasional plague of locust dining on your delectable dahlias.

Just as we did in the concept statement exercise, we're going to begin our planting design with the big picture, then work our way down to the details.

Here's the process I use to select a few dozen plants that will look great and behave well in the garden. It's what I teach in my design classes and it should be enough to get your yard rolling: Imagine that a dump truck just deposited a few thousand ping-pong balls on your driveway, each marked with the name of a plant that grows in your area. The balls need to be sorted and most of them thrown out, so in a little while we'll go grab a few imaginary empty trash cans (four, to be exact) and get to work. But first...

Don't Just Grow There – DO Something

Before we start sorting the ping-pong balls, our first objective is to consider whether any of these plants can do something for you. Yes, it would be nice to have a shrub that would do a midnight run down to the Kwiky-Mart for a pint of Ben & Jerry's, but I'm talking about plants that perform a function. A few ideas:

- Improving your comfort by shading the patio, blocking the wind, trapping dust, allowing welcome sun to warm the breakfast nook in winter
- Hiding a busy street or apartment building
- Controlling erosion, retaining topsoil, filtering pollutants from runoff water
- Producing food, flowers, herbs
- Attracting beneficial insects
- Providing a soft floor for recreation and relaxation
- Composing a drop dead gorgeous focal point

Time to go back to your evolving schematic plan where you've already made decisions about the hardscaping components of the garden. Whatever spaces remain, that's where your hard-working plants go. For instance, if your dining patio is blasted by afternoon sun, that's a logical place for a shade tree between you and the heat source. Got a neighbor's window with a bee-line on your boudoir? Plant something tall and dense enough to give you privacy. Jot down your responses on a copy of the drawing, the same way you did on your Now What? plan from Chapter 1. Now go outside and see if there's anything you missed.

One Size Doesn't Fit All

Plants come in all shapes and sizes, but for the convenience of designing a garden, I divide them into four big groups: Trees, and high, medium and low plants. Time to bring out your trash cans, one for each category, and start lobbing ping-pong balls for Step One of "the great sort-out."

Trees: These are the dominant players in the garden, usually, but not always, having a single trunk and sporting a canopy that starts higher than your head (unless you're more than ten feet tall). We use them for shade, to screen views, as focal points, windscreens, and to add scale to the yard. Logical locations for trees include along paths (but not too close – don't want surface roots messing up the paving), as a green colonnade, at the corners of buildings to frame the architecture, in front of ugly views, and placed throughout the garden for a woodland feeling. When I think trees, I think walls and ceilings of the garden (more kinds of walls in the next category).

High: Anything above eye level when you're standing up, and is not a tree. I think of this category as the "skeleton", or walls, of the garden. These consist mainly of big shrubs, but can include vines supported by a fence, wall or trellis. High plants can be effective screens, take the place of a wall for security, divert the wind, act as garden room dividers, or as the backdrop for a showy bed. Since they form the armature of the garden, I'm more concerned with their structural value and year-round appearance, rather than selecting them solely for the flowers they might produce. When selecting, pay close attention to the leaf color, shape and the overall density of the plants. However, if they do flower, they need to complement the overall scheme.

Medium: Shrubs, ornamental grasses and stout perennials in the knee-high to eye-level range. These are the workhorses in my palette, edging paths, punctuating beds of ground covers and annuals, defining spaces, framing views – and as the "muscle" that fills out planting beds. "Mediums" are most effective in groupings of three or more plants, rather than tossed about here and there. A lot of plants in this category have showy flowers, but since flowers come and go, it's still a good idea to pay attention to all the plants' other attributes. Woody shrubs will usually outlive perennials and need less maintenance, so make good use of them to save time and money.

Low: Prostrate woody plants, herbaceous (soft-tissue) ground covers, smaller perennials, seasonal bulbs, moss and turfgrass. Because these are generally the foreground plants we see up close, I look to them for making a garden sparkle. Floral color is usually a primary concern, but non-flowering plants with other interesting features fit here, too. Smaller plants mean you'll use more of them, and as with the category above, be sure to include some longer-lived woody ground covers in the mix. If the tall and medium plants are the skeleton and muscle of the garden, these are the finery we drape over those forms.

Picking Plants That Thrive

Now you've sorted the truckload of ping-pong balls into four useful categories, but unless you stage a hostile takeover of all your neighbors' garden space, you're gonna have get rid of most of those plants represented by the balls. Call it triage time. You'll do that by rejecting the plants that won't thrive in your garden.

Notice I didn't say grow in your garden, but thrive. I encourage you to pick plants that *want* to be in your yard, not the ones that have to be on life support to make it through the next day.

Every plant has a set of growing conditions that are optimal for healthy growth. Some can tolerate a broad range while others are more finicky. There's no way around it: You've got to do some research. Find authoritative plant encyclopedias for your region, connect with the local Master Gardener program, get recommendations for a reliable nursery, tap into regional plant databases, and put your computer's search engine to work (see Resources).

Four key criteria for choosing plants that thrive are hardiness, sunlight, soil preference and water management. Let's take a look.

 Hardiness refers to a plant's tolerance of frost and low temperatures. The Windmill Palm gracing your cousin's lawn in Atlanta won't stand a chance on your Boulder hillside, nor will your Colorado blue spruce work in his yard. I call it "zone envy" and for the most part, it's something you need to accept. Consult the USDA Hardiness maps in regional plant books and at your local nursery for advice.

 Light intensity affects a plant's quality and survival. Plants that evolved in the understory of tall trees prefer gentle morning light or filtered sun, while those from south-facing bare hillsides require many hours of direct sunlight to do their best. Put a sun lover in deep shade and, if it grows at all, expect long, spindly stems and a weak defensive system. Conversely, plant an Appalachian Bristle Fern on the south-facing wall of your Tucson garage and one summer afternoon you might discover deep-fried kettle chips. Though terminology varies, here's a range of light needs:

- *Full sun* means at least six hours of direct sun. But not all sun is created equal: reflected light off a white wall or the heat-sink effect of nearby black asphalt can boost temperatures significantly.

- *Half sun* means at least four hours of direct sun. However, some plants will be fine in a half-day of cooler morning sun, but will look stressed with the equivalent hours of hotter afternoon sun.

- *Filtered sun / bright shade* means dappled light through a tree canopy, but light enough to read a book without straining.

- *Full shade* means no direct sun; typically found on the north side of a building (unless you're in the southern hemisphere), or under the canopy of a dense tree.

Soil type refers to both the chemical and textural properties of soil. Chemically speaking, we're interested in whether a plant prefers an acidic, alkaline or neutral soil pH. Rather than bore you to tears with a treatise on soil chemistry (waaaaay beyond my pay grade, anyway), let's just say that your best strategy for a hassle-free, sustainable, cheap-to-maintain garden is to stick with plants that are already adapted to the pH of your garden. Most local, in-tune nurseries will stock plants that are appropriate to the pH of nearby gardens, or at least warn you if that little darling you're bringing home might need special attention. When in doubt, look it up.

Soil texture (sometimes called tilth) is determined by the relative amounts of three primary ingredients: clay, silt and sand. The ideal soil type for most gardens is called *loam*, with more or less equal proportions of the following three:

- *Clay soil* is characterized by slow drainage (the kiss of death for many plants), high water-holding capacity, alkalinity, stickiness, high nutrient-holding capacity, and its nearly rock-hard, shovel-busting density when it dries.

- *Silty soil* drains better than clay and has some of its better nutrient-holding features, but compaction can be a problem, especially if the soil is worked when wet.

- *Sandy soil* is easy to cultivate, drains well and warms up quickly in spring. The trade-off is that it loses moisture quickly, meaning more frequent irrigation for many plants, and is not high in nutrients.

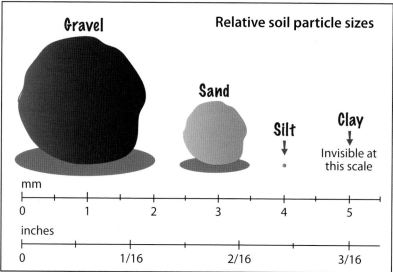

In addition, soil contains organic matter, air, and living organisms.

The good news is that if your soil runs toward either extreme, you can gradually improve its texture and fertility over time. It might sound like snake oil, but adding organic material works wonders for both clay and sand.

If you want to save some coin and your lower vertebrae, take the low-cost, sustainable approach and choose plants that are already adapted to your conditions, since making any significant change to your soil is very difficult.

Water management and your attitude toward irrigation should have a strong influence on the plants you choose for your yard. In arid regions, selecting plants that require dragging a hose around or turning on sprinklers comes at a financial as well as environmental cost. Water is essential for life and I think everyone with a garden and a bathtub needs to think responsibly about how we conserve or squander a limited and unreliable resource.

Like it or not, even the most sustainably conceived landscape will require some amount of supplemental irrigation to get established and make it through dry periods.

Of course, the most sustainable approach is to build your palette around local native plants that have evolved to survive on what the climate naturally provides. And since there are other parts of the world with similar climates to yours, you can include varieties from those regions as well. Where I design, in coastal California's Mediterranean climate, we can use plants from regions of South Africa, Chile, Australia, southern Europe and northern Africa, as well as local natives. This doesn't mean you need to feel guilty about tossing in a few special needs plants, but keeping these at a minimum will make your life a lot simpler and hold your water bill down.

Best advice: Give top priority to plants that you can leave alone without a baby sitter – plants that take care of themselves with only a little TLC from Mom and Dad.

CHAPTER 12

pretty, pretty

Going for "Beautiful"

Now that you've disposed of all the plants that won't serve your needs and have no business in your yard, it's time to round up the survivors and make something beautiful.

Harmony and Contrast

There are entire books written about aesthetics and design, but if I had to pick one concept for all gardeners to understand, it would be the interplay of harmony and contrast, which are opposite sides of the same coin.

The terms refer to how alike or different things are from each other. When I design, these are the first tools I pick up for generating visual interest.

In a yard that takes a mostly harmonious design approach, elements tend to blend well, with no lead performers, nothing yelling, "Hey, look at me!" Harmony applies to the forms, colors, textures, and other visual characteristics of plants or materials. For example, an analogous color scheme (described in this chapter) is all about harmony and might incorporate earth-toned brick paths, natural wood furnishings, terracotta containers, and bronzy foliage accents. Applying this principle at a finer level, you could try using the

same local stone in various forms, like gravel, boulders, and cut blocks. Because they all come from the same source, they'll share the same color and patterning, tying different parts of the garden together.

Contrast, like the black and white squares on a chessboard, leaves no doubt about where one thing ends and the other begins. Used sparingly and strategically, contrast is what makes focal points, like artwork and killer plant combos, stand out in your yard.

A word of caution: Go overboard with contrast and you could end up with a racket of visual noise.

Yards with too much going on suffer from a lack of focus, diagnosed in design circles as One-of-Each-Itis. (This syndrome is the result of frequent trips to the nursery with no recollection of what you bought the week before.) The severity of this condition can range from the politely named "eclectic mix" to "why did you go off your meds?"

Floral Flamboyance

When it comes right down to it, it's flowers that make a garden glow. Our brains are wired for color, a development essential for proto-humans to spot ripe fruit in a tree canopy, or knowing which team to root for in the Neanderthal vs. Australopithecus Olympics. We don't have 6 million cone cells in each eye for nuthin'.

Flowers wake up a garden. And they're sexy, literally. All those petals, stamens, pistils and ovaries aren't just for show; they're how plants reproduce. Their shape, location on the plant, and color determine who pollinates them (birds or bees or butterflies or beetles; wind, too).

Although the plant could care less, one of our main concerns when deciding which flowers to add to our garden boils down to human superficiality: Is it a hottie?

Picking Your Posies

Stylin': Look for examples of the style of garden you're designing – Old World, tropical, urban – and notice how floral color is handled. Are flowers the dominant feature or are they applied with a subtle hand? Does the design use just a few crayons from the box, or is it Jackson Pollack's controlled madness?

The color scheme for a woodland garden should be more muted than a sunny border of a cottage garden, since we're trying to capture the quiet and calm of a forest floor. In desert gardens, flowers are often short-lived, but maximize their likelihood of reproducing by sporting brilliant, neon colors.

Context: Take note of what's surrounding your garden, on your neighbor's property or in a distant vista. A garden that responds to the context around it benefits from "borrowing" colors and forms from the scenery to extend its visual limits.

It's not always necessary to blend in with the surroundings. Unlike a garden with vistas to dramatic mountains, a garden in the midst of a built-up environment can assume virtually any style without contradicting its context. The key thing is to make a conscious decision whether to embrace what's already there, or knowingly contradict it.

Closer to home, literally, context means considering the colors and materials of your exterior house walls. Too often, even someone with a good grasp of color theory succumbs to tunnel vision. As if picking swatches at the local paint store, instead of plants, they succeed in developing a palette of colors that, standing alone, would be attractive. But if they haven't paid attention to the finishes of the house, paving materials, furnishings, or fence, the result could make even a colorblind beagle bury her head in the compost pile.

Color in the garden does not exist in a vacuum – one of your design objectives is to be able to say, "Yes, I meant to do that."

Your color scheme for plants and everything else in your yard should coordinate with house, paving materials, fences and furnishings. I've seen beautifully conceived warm color schemes planted next to a building dominated by cool, blue-gray siding, a design decision that had a jarring effect on the big picture.

Plant form: One more plug for paying attention to more than just the color of the flower petals. Even though our attention is usually on the actual hue of the petals, all the other characteristics of a plant come into play. It's fine to decide you want a splash of bright yellow in the garden. Your final choice shouldn't stop there. Will the color come from a slice of yellow flag *(Iris pseudoacorus)*, with its slender, vertical architecture, a mound of cloud-like forsythia, or a low, buttery spread of pansies? As long as you're picking plants, you might as well exploit as many visible features as possible.

Seasonal changes: As you consider plants for your palette, don't just focus on the appearance at peak bloom. Most plants transform throughout the season, like the way rose blossoms mature into fiery red hips, adding a new dimension to the garden in fall.

Consider how the plant's foliage complements or contrasts with the blossoms. One plant that stymies me (so I don't use it) is Brazilian sky flower, a great screening shrub that blooms, as you would imagine, with sky-blue flowers. It would make a fine backdrop for other plants in the purple to lavender range. But later in the year, the flowers ripen into clusters of tiny orange berries. So do you use it as a cool color addition in spring, but allow for it to transform to the warm component of the bed later in the season? This metamorphosis can change a garden's appearance from month to month, which is what makes garden design so exciting and sometimes perplexing.

Timing is everything. Like with airlines, life would be much easier if flowers had reliable schedules. Wouldn't it be cool if plant labels said: "Flowers appear June 7 at 3:30 p.m., ceasing on July 4, right after the fireworks finish and all your guests leave." Then you could create reliable color combos that match the seasonal table settings on your patio. Do your research and try to find out when each plant is most likely to bloom, and you'll have a great show. You might want to revisit Chapter 7's discussion of the four-season garden.

Color Scheme Categories

Monochromatic refers to a palette of flowers and foliage within a narrow range, such as the pink-red-maroon mix discussed on page 45. You can pick any point on the color wheel and spread out a little in each direction, including adjacent hues, plus tint and shade variations. These simple schemes lend themselves to small gardens, since they're easy on the eye. *Tip:* Tossing in white or gray enriches the range without adding competition.

Experiment with your plant palette. To help visualize future garden beds, create color scheme simulations with clipped images from magazines and the Web... even paint store color chips.

Analogous color schemes expand on the simplicity of a monochromatic approach but broaden the look, using colors adjacent to each other on the color wheel. One of the most sensuous combinations I use starts with violet – a calming, dreamy hue – and pushes the palette over to red, bringing heat and passion to the mix. If I want to cheer the picture up, I'll include lavender and pink tints, or impose a more somber effect with deep shades of burgundy and purple. Using analogous colors makes for more visual interest but still plays it safe by grabbing from a narrow range.

Of course, the same principle works with warm colors. Yellow and orange are close neighbors, which, when combined with their shades (gold and rust), heat up a focal point planting. Expand the palette by one more "wedge" to red, and you've added more BTUs to the burner.

Complementary schemes use polar opposites to generate high contrast. These combinations occur naturally in some plants, like the violet and yellow face of a Johnny-Jump-Up viola. Notice how purple, lavender (purple's tint) and the pure yellow hue seem to jump off the page. Remember our earlier discussion of balance?

This principle applies when you decide on the ratio of warm to cool in a two-part scheme. Note also how little yellow (the warm part of the equation) it takes to balance all the coolness.

The iconic Christmas green and red combo of holly leaves and berries is the epitome of high contrast, as is the fleeting combination of a monarch butterfly feeding on mountain lilac.

More contrast means more visual interest, excitement and drama, so I use this approach with restraint. Unless I'm trying to create a big, bold effect in a grand bed, I tend to limit my use of pure-hue contrasting combos to one or two key locations as focal points. You can continue to play with subtle contrast in adjacent areas, switching to subdued tints, or introducing more neutral colors.

Polychromatic means many colors. It can also translate to Look at All the Crayons My Grandma Gave Me. Are you from the "I just want a lot of color" school of thought? Do you find yourself bringing home any

and every plant as long as they're bright, then scattering them in the garden wherever there's a blank patch of soil?

There's a right way and a wrong way to handle multiple colors. The first is to keep scale and proportion in mind: A small garden can only support so many different plants and colors without resulting in optical anarchy. Strike a balance between saturated and less intense flowers, so their neighbors don't overpower them. Create micro-communities of analogous colors, so each has a bit more impact. By integrating the same concepts of the more organized color schemes discussed earlier, you'll be able to manage more variety without letting things get out of hand.

CHAPTER 13

foliage exploitation

Beyond Flowers

*D*on't get me wrong. I have nothing against flowers. I smell them, I cut them from my garden and indelicately arrange them in empty milk cartons. I've even been known to eat their buds when artichoke season rolls around. But quite frankly, floral color is the last thing I think about when I design. Really. That's because flowers generally aren't in bloom for very long, and most folks don't have the time, budget, or inclination to continually fuss with them.

I tell my design students this story:

> *"Imagine that the moment the lights go off in the house for the night, your garden gnomes come to life. Year-round, they're subjected to scorching heat, torrential rains, and Chico the Incontinent Chihuahua. Now it's break time, and they've only got 'til dawn to be back on the job. They rush down to the all-night pub and commence to pounding down whiskey shots, chased with pints of stout.*
>
> *Careening home in a foul mood, they're really not looking forward to another workday in your garden. So to spite you, they seek out EVERY nascent flower bud that will bloom that day, then pluck and mash them under their teeny black boots."*

My point? Don't count on flowers to give you the garden of your dreams. Plant a garden that will look great whether it's in bloom or not.

If you design your garden as if belligerent, drunken gnomes live there, ready to trample your posies, you'll always have a garden that looks great. Except in the dead of winter when snowdrifts cover some gardens in creamy, white frosting, the "bone structure" of a garden is composed of the forms of the plants – their branches and stems, and foliage. With so many features to play with, why not exploit as many of them as you can to create a framework that provides beauty, harmony, and contrast year-round?

Three things to consider about foliage: leaf color, shape, and plant form

Leaf Color: Leaves come in almost every color imaginable: Silvery white, burgundy blushed, gilded with gold, dark green, yellow green, striped, splotched and stippled. Even on the same plants, leaves can emerge lemon-lime in spring, darken deeply in mid-summer, then catch fire in fall. At Disneyland's Haunted Mansion, there's an all-black-foliage garden around the graveyard! Concentrating on the long-term impact of foliage gives you the most cluck for your plant-purchasing buck.

Leaf Shape: Leaf forms are almost endless: They're succulent, spiraled and snaky; fuzzy, flared and fiercely fanged. Wispy, fringed, undulating, rigid, or succumbing to erectile dysfunction. Mix them up to create strong visual textures, or select similar shapes for a more subtle, harmonious effect.

Plant Form: In addition to the shape, size, color and surface of the leaf, every plant has its own inherent "architecture." (This, of course, assumes that the hedge trimmers are left in the tool shed and your pet goat hasn't been browsing in the garden.)

Two things to consider about *any* plant for your garden: its density and its visual texture.

Density: The principle of mass and space can be applied not only to arranging spaces, but to the visual character of plants as well. A tightly clipped yew hedge is all about mass, not a space to peep through (a great choice if you're starting up a nudist colony). Tall grasses, like Miscanthus, are dense at the base, but open up into a diaphanous curtain, allowing glimpses of other parts of the garden.

Visual Texture: Plants have visual texture that you will immediately experience in your garden, maybe without even realizing why your eye pulled in their direction. Texture has a lot to do with size. Plants with bold, luscious, tropical leaves (coarse-textured canna lily or philodendron) command our visual attention and bring far-away beds into clear view. Plants with small leaves (moss, creeping thyme, baby tears) can be appreciated at close range, but turn into a soft blur at a distance.

There are the emphatically vertical plants like bamboo, Douglas fir, prairie grasses, yarrow and Italian cypress. Fan-shaped plants include New Zealand flax, iris and yucca. Azaleas, lavender, cherry trees and holly take on cloudlike forms. Some plants look like they oozed out of a toothpaste tube, tightly hugging the ground, like Chinese garden juniper, creeping thyme, stone crops and manzanita. Mix 'em, match 'em, have fun!

When analyzing gardens that appeal to you, consider their textural composition and how you can bring that effect to your own garden.

CHAPTER 14

the gentle art of plagiarism

Getting the Best Out of Other People's Gardens

*Y*ou're probably thinking, "So when do I get to stick some plants in the ground?" Trust me, we're getting there.

To this point, I've been throwing a lot of design concepts and vocabulary at you. All this stuff about line and form and harmony and movement and tickling your senses is about to become the fuel that drives the design engine for your own yard.

I don't think you can create the garden of your dreams until you understand what you're dreaming about. The first big step toward unleashing your inner designer is finding inspiration. There are dozens of styles of gardens, hundreds of configurations those gardens can take, and thousands of plants, materials and decorative baubles to choose from.

You need to narrow your options. You need a compelling vision, a Holy Grail to seek. And it all starts by getting your gums scraped.

That's right. For some reason, the best gardening magazines seem to end up in the dentist's waiting room. Their pages are dripping with sumptuous shots of brilliant flowers, alluring walkways sinuously disappearing into fern-festooned grottos, and streams flowing with cool, crystalline water. Perhaps those wily oral hygienists are hoping to take your mind off the pointy tools they're about to cram into your mouth. Of course, if you're a compulsive flosser with great gums, you can always subscribe to the magazines yourself, visit your local library, and scour the Internet for garden images that suit your fancy.

Your chances of creating the garden you dream about increase when you figure out what you like and what you don't. And as I mentioned earlier, what's even more important is understanding why.

But there's a catch. What if the garden that gets you all hot and bothered is growing in the cool, forested regions of the Pacific Northwest and your yard lives in Durham, North Carolina? For certain, you won't be able to simply cut and paste the design, then sand down the edges to make it fit. But you can use that garden to prime your pump. Here's what you do…

"What I Like About You"

Collect photographs of a half-dozen gardens you like, lay them out on the table, and grab a pad and pen. Use books, magazines or images you've captured from the Internet. At the top of the pad, give each garden a title and write "What I Like About You" (one of my favorite 80s tunes by The Romantics). And since there's no such thing as a perfect garden, leave additional space for traits that fall in the "Nice, but" category.

Garden Study #1: Let's assume that the photo on the left turns you on. (It's growing in Santa Barbara, and perhaps has no business in your zone. No worries; it's just here to help find your personal style.) This is essentially a three-plant combo featuring a purple-leaf plum tree (left), New Zealand Tea Bush (right), and Spanish lavender (bottom).

Now we put all that design vocabulary to work.

Notice where your eye goes first. More than likely, it's the dark maroon foliage of the plum. There's something rich and sensual about it – it's in high contrast to the rest of the composition. On your pad, jot down "purple leaves" in your "What I Like..." column. Maybe you've just found a new flavor to spice up your landscape?

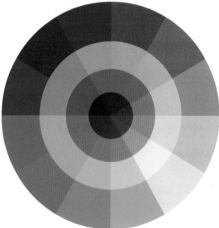

Do the flower colors please your eye? Pale pink plays well with maroon foliage – the tint and shade of red. And the lavender flowers add contrast without coming on too strong. That's because lavender is the tint of purple, the hue just next to red. Make a note: "Strive for subtle range of colors" or "Pink and lavender flowers are yummy together."

What did you just learn? You're attracted to an analogous color scheme, built around red. This scheme expands the color palette by using tints and shades while leaving out the primary hue.

Continue analyzing the composition for "big picture" traits. Perhaps the composition feels a bit too crowded. In the "Nice, but" column write, "Keep plants airy and open."

Let's take one more analytical pass. Notice a range of foliage sizes that add to the contrast – larger leaves on the tree and delicate foliage on the others. The same thought process applies to the density and form of each plant: some solid, some lacier; some mounding and others upright.

Every visual characteristic of each plant is an element you can exploit to generate contrast and harmony.

Garden Study #2: In the photo to the left, we see a very different composition. This striking mash-up features a silky green, variegated form of *Euphorbia ingens*, and I-forgot-my-sunscreen-colored *E. tirucalli* 'Sticks on Fire'. This combo is all about contrast. Other than their shared genus and upright architecture, these two plants couldn't be any less alike: curving planes vs. cylindrical branchlets; creamy vs. smoldering; spiny vs. smooth.

Like it? Dislike it? Pick a column; make a note. How would you apply what you've learned to your own garden vision?

Work your way through the rest of your photos. See if a trend emerges. If most of the designs you like feature wispy, vertical grasses, make room in your palette for a majestic Miscanthus or Calamagrostis. Are you finding that you're drawn to gardens with high proportions of gray foliage? You'll want to build similar plants, appropriate to your zone, into your garden.

The beauty of this exercise is that you'll quickly gain insight into the key elements that work for you.

Put these ideas to work and you'll be rewarded with a garden that reflects your own unique style. Charles Caleb Colton said, "Imitation is the sincerest form of flattery." I'm guessing he had a pretty nice garden.

CHAPTER 15

what, how many & where do they go?

Introducing Your "Core of Four"

Even a seasoned designer (I'm fond of dill weed myself) has a hard time giving birth to a plant palette of a dozen or more varieties off the top of their head. The typical front or back yard will likely include at least a couple of types of trees, a few different background shrubs and vines, and an assortment of smaller plants and flowers. To make this daunting challenge manageable, I've developed what I call the Core of Four. It's a plant selection starter kit consisting of one plant from each of the four categories: tree, high, medium and low, described on pages 84-86. It starts out as a one-column spreadsheet, then eventually expands horizontally as more plants are added.

Here's what the Core of Four is about: Imagine you're only allowed to use four different plants in your garden, but you can have as many of each as needed. Anywhere you require a tree, it's going to be the same one in each location; same goes for the high, medium, and low plants. (Stick with me; I'm not saying you're only allowed four kinds of plants. This is just the first step, identifying the four plants that will be your core.)

Review what you learned about your likes and dislikes from the plagiarism exercise in the last chapter. If you feel like you've come up short on lovable plants, go back to your online and book references and expand your list.

Column 1

TREE

HIGH

MEDIUM

LOW

When you're ready, grab your "What I Like About You" plant list and pick your favorite tree. Pink dogwood *(Cornus florida rubra)*, you say? It's a deciduous, round-canopied tree with strongly horizontal branches, broad, pointed, oval green leaves, and four-petaled pastel pink flowers. For now, this is the tree you'll use throughout your yard – one or more, depending on your space.

Next, you need a tall plant to enclose the yard and create privacy, one that shares a few features with the tree, but not its identical twin. So you choose mock orange *(Philadelphus* x *virginalis)* because it grows 6 to 8 feet tall, has small green leaves shaped like the dogwood's, but displays a weeping habit and has fragrant, showy white flowers.

Your medium plant choice is Japanese barberry *(Berberis thunbergii)*, a dense, mounding, compact, burgundy-foliage plant. Since pink (the dogwood flowers) is the tint, and burgundy is the shade of red, there'll be a bridge between the colors that offsets the change in form.

One plant to go. Maybe you're getting tired of all the rounded forms, so how about a low plant that's vertical, like an ornamental grass? Chinese fountain grass *(Pennisetum orientale)* should do the trick. It's fine-textured and wispy, but when it flowers in spring and summer, the soft brush-like blooms have a pale pink blush, sealing the deal on this narrow, analogous color scheme.

Here's the result: a composition that has enough related parts to look cohesive, but with enough variety to keep from melding into an indistinguishable mass.

Building on Your Core of Four

Now that you have your Core of Four in place, you can build on it, gradually fleshing out a more complex final list. The spreadsheet on this page contains four rows and multiple columns. The first column is filled in, waiting for you to double the number of plants by tackling the next column.

	Column 1	Column 2	Column 3	Column 4
TREE				
HIGH				
MEDIUM				
LOW				

When it comes time to pick your second tree, ignore the high, medium, low plants you already picked and select a second tree to complement the first. My theory is that if tree 1 and tree 2 can form a meaningful relationship, that new tree will make sense with the other three plants in column one.

Watch this…

Column 2

TREE

HIGH

MEDIUM

LOW

There are two approaches: First, you could look for similarities that link your new tree to the dogwood, and some differences.

What about a different variety of dogwood, this one with white flowers? Or, you could go for extreme contrast, like a European Birch *(Betula pendula)* with its upright form, weeping branches, small leaves and white bark. No one will mistake this for another dogwood. Now we're getting somewhere. Cool! You've chosen your second tree! (Sit down. Have a cup of herbal tea. I'm here for you.)

Continue down the list, finding a partner for each of the other first-pick plants from column 1.

High: Philadelphus + Lilac *(Syringa vulgaris)* Why? A touch of purple flowers would expand the palette, and the leaves are a lighter shade of green while sharing a similar shape.

Medium: Berberis + Adagio Maiden Grass *(Miscanthus sinensis 'Adagio')*, a light, airy grass to contrast the density of the Barberry.

Low: Pennisetum + Plantain Lily (Hosta 'Heart and Soul') for a bold, broadleaf accent and a sparkle of chartreuse variegation.

Now you've got one more column on your spreadsheet, expanding your palette to eight plants.

Next, take a shot at filling in column 3, again selecting one more plant for each category. And there you have it – your Core of Four starter kit! You've got a dozen plants, systematically, but artistically selected.

	Column 1	Column 2	Column 3	Column 4

True confession: This system holds up for the first dozen or maybe 16 plants, but you can see how, after a while, the next plant you select from each category is less and less likely to be a good partner for your original selections. But it's enough to get you started on the right path.

Beds...and What Goes On In Them

The next questions are, "How big should my beds be?"... "How many plants will I need to order?" and "How do I arrange them?"

King Size or Twin: How big should my beds be? So many gardens get it backward. They have way too much space dedicated to high maintenance, visually boring lawns and itty bitty, high maintenance, overstuffed beds with plants struggling for water and light.

There are aesthetic as well as practical reasons for making planting beds as big as you can, especially in the front-to-back dimension. Designing in a narrow bed is like trying to conduct a staff meeting with everyone sitting side-by-side on a long bench. The only meaningful interaction that occurs is between folks sitting right next to each other. With narrow planting beds, the only aesthetic "conversation" is between plants that are side by side – fine for a July 4th red, white and blue bunting motif, but that's about it.

However, if the depth of the bed allows enough room for a back row of tall stuff, a mid-ground area for shrubs, theatrical grasses and perky perennials, and a generous leading edge for the little pretties, you've given yourself a canvas where you can create magic.

Assuming you heed my right-plant-in-the-right-place sizing advice, here's how I recommend you allocate the space:

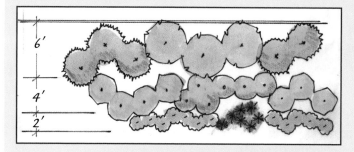

At least six feet of real estate for the back rank: The taller shrubs need space to stretch out in all directions, while keeping their natural form and size.

About four feet for the midsize stuff: This allows room for midsize shrubs, tall grasses, and more complexity.

And at least another two feet in front for the frilly stuff: That would be your spreading ground covers, your masses of tulips to welcome spring, and whatever impulse flowers you can't resist at the garden center.

I'll do the math. That's twelve feet front to back and as wide as your garden can accommodate. Of course, not every yard has this much room, and not every bit of your garden needs to be this complex, but it's a good starting point where you want to add flair.

If you have to economize on space, go vertical: Consider training a vine on the fence to create height without eating up a lot of horizontal real estate. Shop for smaller versions of the plant you like – many plants have a cultivar ending with the name *"compacta"* or *"nana,"* indicating a natural dwarf tendency.

How many plants do I order? Here's my rule of thumb for creating a showy, generous bed in a typical yard:

- Trees – two to three varieties, aiming for some seasonal variation: spring flowers, summer shade, fall foliage.
- High – two to three background plants for each microclimate. You might have two or three for a shaded area under trees, and a few more for a sunny area.
- Medium – between four and six types, mixing shrubs, ornamental grasses and beefy perennials.
- Low – Go wild, as long as you follow the aesthetic principles I laid out earlier, selecting a coherent color scheme and not too many forms. Depending on the style of garden, you might have a few broad swaths of low ground covers punctuated by little "jewel boxes" of a dozen mixed annuals, bulbs and perennials as a focal point. Let the style you've selected guide your ambition.

How do I arrange them? If you've been doing your homework and producing the series of drawings I've described, dig out a copy of your preliminary layout plan and pencil in the approximate configuration of the planting areas. Even if you're not changing any hardscaping in your garden, I still advise that you draw a freehand sketch of the planting areas so you can experiment before you start shopping and digging holes.

We're not building an electron microscope, so "close enough" is good enough. Just make sure it's roughly to scale, like 1/8-inch on the paper equals one foot in real life.

We'll be adding plants to the design using the categories I described in "One Size Doesn't Fit All," pages 84 to 86. Keep in mind that the location and spacing of plants needs to consider the eventual mature size of each one. (See Crimes Against Horticulture, page 121.)

Before you start making dots and circles on the plan, look up each plant in a reliable reference and write down the mature height and spread next to the name. Then, refer back to your site analysis and needs assessment for clues about how plants will help you fulfill your vision for your dream garden – shade, privacy, windbreak, erosion control, etcetera.

Remember, regardless of what your research tells you, plants are not precision instruments and there will always be exceptions depending on lots of variables, like light, soil, fertility and genetics. And not all references agree with each other. Prepare for a few surprises.

Plant Placement: Location, Location, Location

Placing your trees: Trees come first. Draw a plump, juicy dot wherever you think you need a tree. (The dot represents the trunk, not the eventual spread of the canopy.) If you're planting a grove of dogwoods and your research tells you they grow about 16 feet wide, your dots will be that far apart. (If you're drawing at 1/8-inch scale, that's two inches on your plan.) That way, their tips will gently caress, not entangle, when they're all grown up. Think about where they'll cast shade, and how close they are to obstructions and paving. Generally, the roots will spread as wide as the canopy. (Draw the canopy if you like.)

Placing your high and medium plants: For the tall background plants, keep the palette simple, selecting at most, two or three species to fill the big spaces. These are the supporting actors and too much variety will become a distraction for the smaller workhorse plants in the middle and foreground. Plant multiples of each in groupings, the way Mother Nature does it.

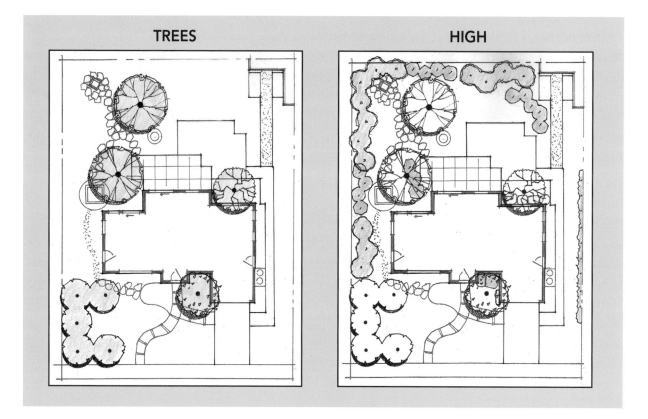

TREES   HIGH

I'm okay with packing background plants a little bit tighter than their mature size if your objective is a dense screen, but not closer than 75 percent of their full spread. For example, although some forms of boxwood *(Buxus sempervirens)* can grow 10 feet wide and high, you can pack them in at 7 or 8 feet apart. If you're really impatient, I give you permission to start twice as many as you eventually need at 5 feet spacing, then cull out every other one as they converge. Thinning the stand makes maintenance easier in the long run.

However, if your shrubs or big ornamental grasses will be standing out in the open where their inherent natural form is an asset, leave extra space around them. Also, think about other plants nearby and whether you want a dense, slightly overgrown mass, or prefer a bit of breathing room between masses.

Your objective at this point in the design is to create attractive layers of plants for an interesting visual composition. As you work your way toward the viewer, it's fine to increase the number of varieties in the middle range, adding complexity and seasonal variation. When in doubt, look at examples of the style you're creating and let that be your guide.

Placing your low plants: Whatever ground is left will be filled with low growing plants (or in some cases, an attractive swath of mulch or decorative rock). I find it hard to control myself at this stage, because there are so many cool ground covers and perennials with lots to contribute.

Think of low perennials as a transition from your medium shrubs, blending them into the color scheme you've chosen and considering how their form and foliage can expand the complexity of the design, or harmonize with the motif you've established. Here's a good place to introduce bright, variegated leaves, if you haven't already.

Ground covers (prostrate plants that spread by clumping or runners) are used in the foreground of the bed. When used in broad swathes, they can be a stabilizing element in the grand scheme and give the eye a rest. Or plant them between stepping-stones, but be careful to select well-behaved, fine-textured ones, lest they overrun your path.

MEDIUM-LOW

The ultimate low-growing plant is a grass lawn, that emblem of suburbia. Do you really need a silly patch of water-hogging, time-consuming lawn to store your pole vaulting equipment? When you have a chance, join me in Appendix E for my rather strong feelings about turfgrass, "Murder Your Lawn."

Bringing Up Baby: the post-partum garden

There's a statistical possibility that the crew from Publishers Clearing House will march up your driveway with a giant check, evaporating your money concerns. Until that day comes, I'm guessing that you're keeping an eye on how much you spend, including in your new garden.

I think it's critically important, during the planning stage, to consider not only the initial cost of design and installation, but also the actual "life cost." It's sort of like being pregnant (which I haven't actually tried, because I hear it makes your clothes fit poorly for a few months): If all you're thinking about is how long the delivery is going to take, and not looking down the road at saving for little Zoe's orthodontist and a college education, you've only got a small piece of the big picture on your radar.

Applying that same idea to your yard, I've seen statistics showing that the cost of installing a garden is only 20% of the real life cost. The other 80% gets spent on water, fertilizer, tools, trash hauling, repairs, and maintenance hours. One study (an ongoing project – The Garden/Garden Project – by the city of Santa Monica, California) compared a community's traditional "mow and blow" gardens with sustainably design ones. The Earth-friendly gardens, featuring efficient irrigation systems, and regionally adapted low-water-using, properly spaced plants, used 90% less water. These landscapes generated one-third less yard waste and required 20, rather than 80, hours of maintenance per year. As they say in Detroit, your "mileage" may vary, but you can see how the choices you make now can save you time, money, and, quite possibly, a trip to the chiropractor.

The Numbers Speak for Themselves

Traditional Landscape			Sustainable Landscape		
57,000	670 Pounds	80 Hours	6,000	250 Pounds	15 Hours
Water	Yard Waste	Maintenance Hours	Water	Yard Waste	Maintenance Hours

Based on The Garden/Garden Project, a study by the city of Santa Monica, California

Be Plant Smart: I'll say it once again: If you don't want to be a slave to your garden, pay close attention to selecting plants that won't outgrow the space you put them in – it's a black hole that sucks away your time and money. Gardening should be enjoyable and invigorating. I don't know about you, but standing atop a six-foot ladder wielding a screaming, smelly, finger-threatening power hedge trimmer ranks pretty low on my fun scale. I'd much rather spend my morning picking through cool new plants at the nursery and showing them off in an artistically arranged container on my front porch.

I've talked about the importance of well-spaced plants; another advantage is that the less you have to prune them, the less greenwaste you'll pay to have hauled away.

Be Water-Wise: For keeping money in your pocket, smaller water bills should be a no-brainer. Plant natives and locally adapted plants that don't need supplemental water. Use drip irrigation to deliver water only to the root zone. If you have a spray system, invest in state-of-the-art rotor nozzles that deliver water only to the plants, instead of watching it drift to your neighbors' gardens on the slightest breeze. And check out smart controller technology – devices that receive real-time weather information, turn off when it's raining and then crank themselves up a notch when it's hot and dry. You'll not only consume only as much water as the plants require, but you'll lessen the risk of having to replace those that didn't get what they need when they need it. And pile on the mulch to reduce evaporation, prevent erosion and cut down on weeding.

End Chemical Dependency: Planting a diverse array of natives and beneficial insect attractors means fewer pests, which in turn means savings on sprays and equipment – and even more important, not having all those toxic potions on your tool shed shelves. That's good for you, your family, your neighbors, and the environment.

Good Clean Dirt: I'm getting to this last, but a well balanced, healthy, thriving garden starts with the most basic ingredient: your soil. The cheapest, easiest thing you can do for your garden is to make your plants' roots happy, an improvement that pays you back for decades. I've already touched on how incorporating compost into your beds benefits many types of soil, and how it leads to a living, breathing biological system that's essential to healthy plant growth.

While you're at it, turn your leaf rake into a hood ornament and pick up a cultivator. All that nutrient-filled organic material should be returned to the soil, just the way natural forests recycle their leaves into fertilizer for the trees. It really doesn't make sense to dispose of the free stuff, then drive to the store for a bag of chemical fertilizer to replace what you just took away. And while you're scratching the leaves back into the soil, you'll prevent weed seeds from sprouting and making it easier for water to penetrate.

Along with improving the soil, institute best management practices.

Before and during construction – especially if you're building a new house or doing an extensive renovation – compaction and soil pollution are your greatest enemies.

Some things to be aware of:

- Trucks and heavy equipment on bare soil squeeze out pore space, making root and water penetration more difficult, and depriving the complex web of subterranean life of the air and gases it requires.

- Another byproduct of allowing your future garden to be used for construction staging is that a surface crust inevitably forms, increasing run-off and erosion.

- Be vigilant about how and where masons, painters, and concrete delivery trucks "clean up." Most of them think that soil is "just dirt" and they thoughtlessly dispose of their spoils wherever it's most convenient. If your architect and superintendent are doing their jobs, they'll include and enforce rules that protect your precious soil and existing plants.

- And lastly, protect your important trees! I strongly recommend erecting temporary fencing around the outer circumference of the branch tips, to keep out any harmful activities from under the drip line.

Crimes Against Horticulture:
When Bad Taste Meets Power Tools

Lots of gardens I see are either misguided or they outright suck. If they were simply ugly, I might not get so enraged as I drive through suburban neighborhoods and strip malls.

I know that, ugly is in the eye of the beholder and my revulsion is my own doing. Perhaps after four decades in the world of gardens, my expectations are too high. True, not every garden has to look like a magazine cover. That's the danger of knowing my subject so well – my standards become more refined and expectations rise, setting me up for unavoidable disappointment and, in rare cases, rabid frothing.

But when you combine ugly and avoidable environmental impacts, I'm sorry, but that's inexcusable. We're beyond the point where curb appeal alone can be the Holy Grail. While we're at it, can we also consider how our gardens affect our neighbors, our communities, and the planet?

I've already shared my deep belief that all gardens, regardless of their climate zone or style, can and should be beautiful, useful, and sustainable. It's really not that hard to pull off. All it takes is an appreciation of beauty, a think-before-you-plant mindset, and an understanding of how gardens connect to the rest of the planet.

Crimes Against Horticulture is the result of my morbid fascination with what motivates people to butcher and dominate plants – to force them into submission, carving them into hockey pucks, toilet bowl brushes, or satellite dishes.

The worst of these heinous acts appear to be an outgrowth of a professional "plant janitor" who bids too many hours for a job and has to look busy for the client. So out come the razor-sharp, casehardened steel 200-horsepower, fuel-injected hedge trimmers, and the battle ensues. Gimme a break…gardening requires artistry as much as it calls for brawn. Gardens should be little slices of nature, not places for control freaks to impose their compulsion for order on our plants.

Before you turn the page, be warned: The images you are about to see have the power to instill deep trauma in those who love real plants. Brace yourself for shock and awe.

When the aliens arrive, they'll understand this coded alphabet

AARGH!!!

Grow-it-yourself, high-fiber ice cream cones

If France ever declares war on the US, it's because some numb-nut pruned French lavender into an aromatherapy recliner

conclusion

See what you've gone and done? You've poked your nose into the brain of a landscape architect and witnessed the turmoil within.

If I did my job well, some good stuff has rubbed off and you're in a better position to grapple with the pleasures and challenges of creating a beautiful, supportive, easy-on-the-planet space for living.

If you only take away one big AHA! from the time we've spent together, I hope it's the awareness that there's a process you can rely on to create your ideal outdoor space. Keep your eyes peeled for me as I work my way around the country, giving talks and teaching workshops. I'm always learning new things and would love to continue sharing them with you.

Your pal,

Billy Goodnick

appendix a

To Draw or Not To Draw

(Do I *really* need to draft a working plan? Some tips that can help)

Measuring your property and drafting a plan for your new garden can be a chore. The reasons for putting your ideas on paper vary widely, but I think that it's worth some effort for most projects.

For a simple planting makeover you can get by with pacing off the overall dimensions of your yard, borrowing a sheet of your kid's graph paper and drafting a "close enough" representation of the space. The value of putting even a simple planting plan on paper is this: You can experiment with different configurations for beds, paths, outdoor rooms, and then know how many plants you'll need to purchase and how much square footage to devote to hardscape. But it's not absolutely essential that you do that.

For construction-intensive, dust-raising overhauls the level of graphic description increases. You'll need a higher degree of accuracy when it comes to knowing how much flagstone to order, how many feet of drain line you'll need, and whether you'll have enough space for that soaking tub. I'm not promising to make you into an accomplished drafter; I'm offering a few guidelines and thumbnails to get you started.

1. Research
Get all the reliable information you can about your property: architect's plans, assessor's maps, deed maps, treasure maps, whatever. They will save you a good deal of time. Be sure they are accurate and reflect the current conditions. There may have been alterations to the building and surroundings since the plans were done, so double-check a few critical dimensions.

2. Materials – See Home Design Studio (Appendix B)

3. "Flintstone" Measurement Methods (crude but useful):

The intricacies of measuring and drafting a landscape plan are beyond the scope of this book, but there's lots of information online and in more detailed garden design books. If your project will include a lot of construction, grading and drainage, or if you're working near your property line and there's even a remote question regarding its location, it pays to hire a land surveyor to prepare an accurately scaled drawing.

If your project falls short of that, use these guidelines to get you started:

Measure the house itself, using a 100-foot tape and have an assistant hold the zero-end at the corners of the house. Note all the ins and outs of the façade, plus windows, doors, down spouts, utilities, gates, plumbing fixtures, etc.

To find the locations of walks, patios, and other stuff, measure them in relation to the house. If they're parallel and perpendicular to the exterior walls, it's pretty straightforward. Basically, you're creating a grid off the walls of the house. If there are freeform curves, such as the border of your lawn, lay an imaginary grid over the space, marking regularly spaced points using stakes or nails wrapped with ribbon as the spots where you take measurements.

Mark the location of major trees. But don't obsess about masses of flowers and shrubs. There's a good chance you'll be changing a lot of those.

Transfer the dimensions you gathered onto a large (24-inch by 36-inch) sheet of paper using graph paper or an architect's scale. Leave plenty of room around the edges for notes, a list of supplies and your plant list.

Note any significant landform changes: top and bottom of slope, drainage swales, rock outcroppings. If the topography is complex, hire a professional land surveyor. But simple topographic variations can be measured using a string-line level.

When you're done, you'll have a plan like this.

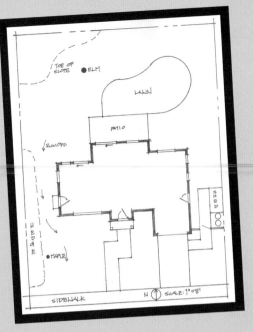

My final words of wisdom about drawing (at the risk of repeating myself)

Start in pencil until you know you've got everything right; you can ink the base map later. The key thing is to keep the drawing simple. The more of the existing landscape you draw in your base sheet, the harder it is to imagine a different garden than the one you have. Lastly, take that final drawing to a copy shop and make multiple copies of the drawing, preserving your original base map in case you need a clean copy later.

Depending on the complexity of the project, you might create some or all of the drawings listed below. You've met most of these throughout the book, in greater detail.

The first three can be rendered on tracing paper laid over the base map:

- **Site analysis:** a simple sketch of what you've observed about the site and how you feel about it
- **Now What?:** your "brain dump" after completing the site analysis and needs assessment
- **Bubble diagrams:** three or more, drawing on tracing paper over a base sheet

Others that can get you where you need to go:

- **Preliminary layout:** general shapes of living spaces, fences, paths, focal points, walls, planting beds, drawn accurately to scale
- **Preliminary plant massing:** trees, high, medium, low
- **Final hardscape layout:** refining the forms, materials, and dimensions
- **Final planting design:** drawing circles representing the mature sizes and spacing of each plant
- **Irrigation and lighting:** pipe/conduit size and location, sprinkler and fixture choices and locations
- **Construction details:** zoomed-in drawings of built features, like retaining walls, paving, irrigation, patio structures, pools, etc.

appendix b

Home Design Studio

(All the tools you need... it's not rocket science)

This list of tools and supplies should be enough to get you through your design project. Most art supply stores will carry the drafting-related stuff and your local hardware store is the place to stop for the measuring tools. If you're handy with a computer and have software that makes it easy to draw to scale, you can try your hand at it, but printing the large sheets that are the most practical for landscape designs can be hard to come by. When it doubt, keep it simple.

Drafting table or flat space to lay out drawing and tools

Drawing Media:

- 24" by 36" sheets of vellum paper, ⅛-inch grid (2-3 sheets)
- 8½" by 11" pad of graph paper and clipboard
- Roll of tracing paper 12" and 24" wide
- Drafting or lightly sticky masking tape

Drafting Supplies

- T-square or table-mounted parallel drafting bar
- Pencils (hard and soft lead) and eraser
- Pens, varying point widths
- Colored pencils or markers
- Architect's scale (not engineer's scale)
- Circle template (other shapes also helpful)
- Drawing compass
- Drafting triangles
- French curves

Measuring Supplies

- 100-foot and 30-foot measuring tapes
- Screwdriver to anchor "zero-end" of tape, or assistant
- Digital camera, computer and printer
- String-line level and string, or water-tube level tool

appendix c

Do It Yourself... Or Hire a Pro?

This might be one of the hardest questions to answer, especially if you're keeping an eye on the checkbook.

In the introduction, I made a promise: I'd either make you into a better designer or turn you into an informed consumer should you decide to work with professionals. I'm doing my best to enlighten you to the design tricks the pros keep in their magic bags, but sometimes it pays to know when you're in over your head. I'll start with considerations to mull over before you pick up that drafting pencil. Then I'll give you a quick look at the people you can team up with to get the perfect project.

Consider how much time you're willing to put into designing your garden and your ability to sort through complex and sometimes conflicting solutions. Think about whether you have the creative and artistic ability to satisfy your vision.

Gardens come all levels of complexity and sophistication. For some folks, their dream garden might consist of no more than a comfy place to scarf down a grilled sausage (just sauerkraut and mustard for me), a path to the veggie garden, and a sunny, colorful flower border. There's nothing wrong with deriving pleasure from simple things.

We're all busy and there's lots to deal with in designing a garden: measuring and photographing, analyzing all the opportunities and constraints, deciding on a style, exploring concepts for each space. Then there are the nuts and bolts issues related to grading, retaining walls, construction details and irrigation plans.

Can you do it all yourself or will you need help?

Questions to ask:

- Are you in a hurry to complete the design or will this be a long-term project? You might be at this for a few months. If your project is complex enough to require permit submittals and reviews – and you're handling that yourself – you'll need to be available during weekday work hours.

- Do you have a dedicated space where you can work on the design without forfeiting the use of the dining room table?

- How will you deal with differences of opinion within the family? I've never done a project that didn't end up being a series of trade-offs and compromises; can you be an impartial player?

- Are you the creative, imaginative type who can generate a range of solutions, dream up interesting forms and material combinations, and develop a pleasing color palette? To use a food analogy, some of us can pull five random ingredients from the pantry and create a feast; others call out for pizza.

- Are you a good researcher and manager of details? Depending on the scope of your project, you might need to deal with zoning restrictions, design review guidelines and building permit submittals to assure you've complied with the rules. Asking the right questions, understanding the answers, and then integrating that information into the design saves time, money and frustration later. A few more points to ponder…

- How are your plant skills? Planting design is more than decorating; plants need to be matched to their location in order to thrive. Selecting the right plant for the right place will save you countless hours of maintenance.

- Are you comfortable converting your design ideas to paper? You don't have to be able to draw like Da Vinci, but sketching your initial thoughts, then organizing your ideas into a plan and experimenting with different configurations will help you find the best solution. When it comes time to build, a scaled, detailed drawing of all the construction elements is essential.

REALITY CHECK:

There's no guarantee that designing or building a project yourself will save you money.

Who Ya Gonna Call?

If your project will be mainly about planting, I'm sure this book will give you the info you need to get to the finish line. But if your ambitions include a combination of extensive planting as well as site planning and construction, you'll want to know about the landscape universe's "food chain" – the various professions and services available to you, and exactly what they do.

A few more questions to mull over, to help you see what the best fit might be.

- Will you need to submit plans to a review board?
- Will any of the construction work require building permits?
- If you're not a do-it-yourselfer, will you want to shop around for bids or do you know a reliable contractor with good references?
- If multiple building trades are involved, how do you feel about coordinating everyone's work?

There are many professions that play a role in the design, permitting, installation and care of a landscape. The consultants or builders you hire vary with the complexity of the project. Knowing who to team up with and why can save you heaps of money and aggravation in the long run. Here's a look at the services you might want to use.

On the Creative Side

Landscape Architect: Licensed by most states, they usually have a college or post-graduate degree.

What they design: site planning, hardscaping, irrigation, grading/drainage, planting, decor, lighting, water features, planting (though not all are strong in horticulture). They often act as primary project manager, coordinating the services of subconsultants...

Engineering subconsultants:
- Mechanical engineer: pumps, sumps, gas, sewer
- Geotechnical/soils engineer: soil stability, drainage
- Structural engineer: retaining walls, buildings
- Civil engineer: drainage, grading, roadways, paving
- Electrical engineer: service upgrade, new outlets

Other subconsultants:
- Architect: cabanas, special buildings, sheds, specialty carpentry
- Irrigation designer: large scale, complex projects
- Pool designers: swimming pools, spas, waterfalls, water features
- Lighting designer: complex projects
- Biologist: environmental reports and construction oversight
- Horticulturist: planting design and plant selection

Landscape Designer: Unlicensed, although some states offer certification; anyone can call themselves a landscape designer. Some have professional affiliations and are tested and peer reviewed, for example, by the Association of Professional Landscape Designers (APLD).

Usually limited to residential work, they can design and lay out hardscape and structural features, but cannot specify construction or engineering details. They are often strong in horticulture, and usually less expensive than a landscape architect.

Design/Build Company (full service contractor): The contractor is allowed to act as a landscape architect or designer on projects that the contractor then installs. This is one stop shopping, though the contractor generally prohibits shopping around the design for additional bids.

Landscape Contractor: Some offer design services; usually untrained in design, no degree or certification. Check with past customers regarding design ability.

Garden Builders

General contractor: Works on projects with a high percentage of construction; might team with landscape contractor as subcontractor.

Landscape contractor: Works on most aspects of landscape construction. Sometimes hires subcontractors: masonry, concrete, carpentry, electrical; planting and irrigation.

Landscaper: The main focus is general landscape installation. Not licensed and can be a crap-shoot; be sure to check references.

Gardener: The main focus is garden maintenance, planting and basic irrigation. No particular certification required; skills vary widely.

Specialty contractors: They can assist with DIY projects, paving, masonry, electrical, tile, pool/spa, etc.

Others

Horticulturist/garden coach: Helps develop plant palette and advise on plant installation and care.

Permit processing service: Deals with submittals, reviews, permits, review boards.

appendix d

Resources

Online Design Ideas
- Photo sharing sites: Houzz.com, Pinterest.com, Flickr.com, Picassa.com
- Magazine websites: *Fine Gardening* (FineGardening.com), *Garden Design* (GardenDesign.com), *Sunset* (Sunset.com), *Southern Living* (SouthernLiving.com), *Martha Stewart Living* (MarthaStewart.com), *Better Homes and Gardens* (www.bhg.com), Leaf (LeafMag.com)

In-Print Design Ideas
- Local bookstore garden shelves
- Local library magazines and books

Horticultural Resources
- Regional Master Gardener programs and web sites; usually part of university extension
- University extension programs
- National and regional horticultural societies (www.ahs.org)
- Botanic gardens and arboreta visits and websites (www.publicgardens.org)
- Horticultural websites: DavesGarden.com, Monrovia.com, Blotanical.com, #gardenchat blog and #gardenchat on Twitter, Annie's Annuals, High Country
- Colleges and universities with horticulture programs
- Regional flower and garden shows, state fairs, and educational seminars
- Garden club tours (www.gcamerica.org)
- Garden Conservancy Open Days tours (www.gardenconservancy.org)

Professionals

- American Society of Landscape Architects (www.asla.org)
- Association of Professional Landscape Designers area chapter (www.apld.com)
- State Landscape Contractors Associations (www.lawnandlandscape.com/AssociationSearch)
- American Nursery & Landscape Association (www.anla.org)

Accessibility and Universal Design

- Therapeutic Landscape Network (www.healinglandscapes.org)

In addition to these resources, the world is bursting with garden lovers who graciously share their knowledge. Facebook and Yahoo have dynamic, helpful discussion groups; garden blogs are everywhere, Twitter's #gardenchat group is a wealth of information. There are TV and radio shows, and don't overlook the great advice you can pick up from certified nursery people at your local independent garden center.

appendix e

Murder Your Lawn

(The siren song of the perfect lawn)

I'm biased. I live in a place where lawns have no business existing, at least not if you're concerned about protecting precious water. Most of SoCal gets between 15 and 20 inches of rain per year, the majority of it falling in the winter. Around Phoenix or Boise, you're lucky if you get half that. But in every neighborhood you go, there's that monotonous patch of green, sucking up life-giving water. Most of the popular cool-season grasses (fescues, Kentucky bluegrass, perennial rye) need about 1-½ inches per week during the growing season. If that liquid isn't falling from the sky on a regular basis, it's coming from somewhere else where it could be serving a higher use.

I don't think it's risen to the level of an unhealthy obsession, but I'll admit that my pulse doubles and my adrenal glands kick into hyper-drive when I see water being wasted. I don't care if it's a poorly adjusted sprinkler system sending whitewater rapids down the gutter, or some lazy bonehead hosing one leaf across a driveway; it drives me nuts. Whether due to ignorance or indifference, there's no excuse.

Perhaps you live where enough rain falls throughout the growing season that you rarely irrigate. I'm happy for you, but you're not off the hook when it comes to environmental impacts. Lawns that are maintained in traditional ways have significant negative effects on the environment and the health of your family and community:

- Air pollution from gas-powered mowers and edgers puts out at least 5 percent of the air pollution in the U.S., emitting carbon dioxide, carbon monoxide, sulfur, and other airborne junk. (That's from the EPA.)

- Most homeowners and lawn professionals apply far more petroleum-based fertilizer than needed for an attractive lawn. What isn't used by the plants percolates into the water table or flows to creeks, lakes and beaches.

- The big national brands try to make you believe that your neighbors are talking about you behind your back if your lawn doesn't look like a PGA putting green. You're persuaded to bombard your yard with synthetic pesticides, the majority of which actually drift off-site, causing water and air pollution, harming wildlife and beneficial insects, and contributing to diseases like cancer, birth defects and severe skin reactions.

- Although some enlightened communities have greenwaste recycling programs, most of the clippings from your weekend assaults end up in a landfill. (A 1/3-acre lawn can produce as much as *2 tons* of clippings in a year.) This is useful material that should be recycled into the soil.

- And since most folks depend on gas-powered mowers, there's the unceasing din of mowers (and other power tools) drowning out the birds, frogs and rustling trees.

Sure, kids and dogs gotta play on something soft and it's not likely you'll carpet your garden with old mattresses. If you really have a compelling reason to keep a lawn – for me, that only includes recreation – at least care for it in the most benign, planet-friendly way.

Did you know that setting your mower a half-inch higher in the summer conserves water by encouraging longer grass, which will shade and cool the ground? Or that adjusting your irrigation controller to cycle on a few times, but for shorter periods, assures that water sinks down where the roots grow, instead of running off?

If you're in a water-challenged part of the country – and with the global climate sending us new surprises every day, yours might be next – check with your local water purveyor for techniques and gizmos to help you save water and lower your water bill.

Mowers: What else do I hate about lawns? The noise, the stink, and the danger to life and limb posed by power tools. A few manufacturers have redesigned and retooled their human-powered push mowers. At a recent garden show I "test drove" a manually operated reel mower that looks like something from a sci-fi movie. It's quiet, amazingly easy to push (self-sharpening blades won't "choke" on stubborn turf), and the only thing you smell is the aroma of fresh baked bread (okay, fresh chlorophyll). Another mowing innovation is a powered mulching mower, which holds the cut grass in suspension long enough to pulverize it into tiny pieces that invisibly fall back onto the lawn. These little bits act as an insulating mulch layer that gradually decomposes, reducing evaporation, supplying nitrogen and eliminating the need for disposal.

Set your mower a bit higher in hot weather, so the blades of grass shade the soil. And follow tried and true water conservation techniques, like rotor nozzles that deliver water right to the grass instead of drifting off on a breeze.

Sustainable lawn care resources: Visit SafeLawns.org, a most enlightening website, advocating for natural lawn care and grounds maintenance. Paul Tukey founded this not-for-profit organization in 2006. He learned about a community in Canada that started a movement that eventually led to a ban on lawn and garden chemicals through much of Canada, and inspired similar laws in parts of the U.S. Also, check out LawnReform.org, a coalition of environmental writers and activists (including me) serving up information and resources about appropriate, sustainable lawn care.

Who needs a lawn? Throughout cities and suburbia, people are ignoring the siren song of the "perfect" lawn. They're growing food, creating cozy courtyards to relax and entertain, planting rain gardens to capture and harvest rainfall, and creating wondrous "biology labs" where their kids experience nature up close and personal. Leading authors in this adventure include Evelyn Hadden's *Beautiful No-Mow Yards: 50 Amazing Lawn Alternatives*, and John Greenlee's inspirational *The American Meadow Garden: Creating a Natural Alternative to the Traditional Lawn*.

acknowledgments

Some people achieve greatness because of their upbringing. If I ever achieve greatness, it will be in spite of my parents' gardening prowess. My mom, Lovely Linda of Lemona is remembered for the tacky plastic flowers she wrapped around the "boring" jade plant in our yard. I thank my pop, Irv, who wouldn't know one botanical name from another, for referring to blue fescue as "hairy balls," much to my brother's and my delight, and for schlepping me to all my drumming gigs.

David, my big brother who somehow avoided decapitating me as we hacked Algerian ivy from the hell strip.

IN THE WORLD OF GARDENS AND PLANTS: Bob Cunningham, giving me my first job in a landscape architect's office • Gary Dwyer, showing me another way of seeing • Pam Andrews, sharing her deep design knowledge and friendship • Owen Dell, for his vision, twisted humor and passion • John Brookes and Penelope Hobhouse, conceiving books that inspire and clarify • Sunset Western Garden Book and its creators, an invaluable resource that continually inspires • City of Santa Barbara, letting me design their parks for two decades • Grant Castleberg, allowing me to play with "Alice" • CJD 3 and the Dirt Bag Gardeners, convincing me to get my butt out of the trenches and back to school • Virginia Hayes and Randy Baldwin, sharing their horticultural wisdom • The visionary botanists, horticulturists, landscape architects, designers, and planners, leaving a legacy in Santa Barbara • Bonsai masters George Yamaguchi and John Naka, kindling my love affair with plants before I knew it • "Jonstance" Thayer, letting me transform their yard into the garden of our dreams • Decades of swell clients, providing classrooms where I could experiment • The Buffalo Gals, making all-nighters at Cal Poly memorable.

IN THE WORLD OF WORDS: Nancy Shobe, who said, "You have a voice" • Barbara Lanz-Mateo, putting my first words in print • Nan Sterman, suggesting I join Garden Writers Association • Peter and Sue Sklar, tolerating my silliness at Edhat.com • Debra Prinzing, supporting, honing, showing the way • Lynne Andujar, polishing this rough stone • Debra Lee Baldwin, Amy Stewart, and Susan Harris, eager to share their vast knowledge and teaching writer's survival skills • Shirley Bovshow, putting my mug on the little screen • Steve Aitken, Kate Frank, Ann Straton, Michele Gervais and Ruth Dobsevage, my Fine Gardening family, transporting me from Twitter to a national audience • Marcia Meier, deciphering the writing universe • All my hard-working, generous, curious writing family at The Business of Garden Writing Facebook page • Paul Kelly, you said "This should be a real book" • Cathy Dees, my gentle editor, you make me look like I know what I'm doing • Holly Rosborough, magically making my words come to life on the page.

GOOD FRIENDS, ALWAYS THERE: Rob, Jill and Sadie • Rotten Robby, Joel, Doug and Rachel, helping me lay the funk down • Ellie, Anya and Matt • Maury, Yvonne and Neecy, my birthday sisters • Steve Jobs and the people who designed my MacBook Pro and my Panasonic DMC-ZS3 camera • All musicians, all over the world.

photo credits

I gratefully acknowledge the following for the use of their images on these pages:

Bomanite Corporation: 74 bottom
Shirley Bovshow: 124
City of Santa Barbara: 89, 118
TC Conner: 60 top, 69 right
Shawna Coronado: 54
Jane Gates: 69 left, 90
Lin Goodnick: 142
Evelyn Hadden: 57 bottom, 84 top, 95, 108 2nd down
Jack Kiesel: 67
Holly Lepere (Grace Design): 16 bottom, 17, 48, 66,
    77 bottom, 84 middle & bottom, 91, 136

Chris Lindsey: 110 3rd down
Pam Penick: 12, 65, 68
Debra Prinzing: 7, 21, 25 bottom
Genevieve Schmidt: 43, 97 bottom
Trevor Shirk: 118 bottom
Rebecca Sweet: 96 bottom, 128
Barbara Wise: 18, 96 bottom
Proven Winners: 108 3rd down, 110 2nd and 4th
Trex Company: 75
Wikimedia stock photo, Colibri1968: 99

Many of my photos were taken at these public gardens:

Bloedel Reserve, Bainbridge, Washington: xvi, 42,
    86 bottom center & right, 101 bottom left & right
Cornerstone Gardens, Sonoma, California: 15 bottom, 41
Filoli, Woodside, California: 45 bottom
Flora Grubb Gardens, San Francisco: 106
Ganna Walska Lotusland, Santa Barbara, California:
    opposite table of contents, 13 top
Huntington Library, Art Collection and Botanical Gardens,
    San Marino, California: 85 top right

Indianapolis Museum of Art: 50, 85 top center
Portland Japanese Garden: 13 bottom, 85 top left
San Francisco Botanical Garden: 25 top, 49, 79
Santa Barbara Botanic Garden: 40 top
The United States Botanic Garden,
    Washington, D.C.: 100 lower right
The United States National Arboretum, Washington, D.C.: 38
Wegerzyn Gardens, Dayton, Ohio: xviii (preceding p. 1), 40

Garden Designers whose work appears in Yards:

Shawna Coronado: 54
Topher Delaney at Cornerstone: 41
Marcia Donahue: 68
Hope Noël Fidiura: 54
Billy Goodnick: 8, 47 bottom, 16 middle, 76 top,
    86 lower left, 92, 96 top, 98, 102 top, 108 bottom
Margie Grace – Grace Design: (see Holly Lepere, above):
    16 bottom, 17, 48, 77 bottom, 84 middle & bottom, 91, 136
John Greenlee: 15 bottom, 139

Arianna Jansma: 60 bottom, 93
Jack Kiesel: 67
Kris Kimpel: 27 bottom
Fujitaro Kubota: 42 bottom, 86 bottom center,
    101 lower right
Rebecca Sweet: 128
Susan Van Atta, Van Atta Associates:
    10 top, 28, 34, 56, 72, 94 bottom

If I have omitted credit for any photographer or garden designer, my apologies; it was unintentional.
Please let me know, and I will credit you in further editions of the book.

about the author

BILLY GOODNICK is an award-winning landscape architect and design coach based in Santa Barbara. He teaches design at the local college, writes and blogs for Fine Gardening magazine, and is a contributor at Houzz.com. A witty, sought-after lecturer, Billy has created some of the most beautiful, environmentally responsible gardens in Southern California – large and small – and has taught his successful techniques to thousands of people. In a previous incarnation, Billy was an in-demand studio and touring drummer in Los Angeles, but laid down his sticks after falling under the enchantment of bonsai, his gateway drug to horticulture. But you'll still find him laying down a solid groove in clubs around town.

Learn more about his garden universe at www.billygoodnick.com